Advance Praise

"Michele Sharp, a novice sailor when she begins this adventure, summons up courage, conviction and tenacity as she sets out on a 109-day, 5000-mile journey by water from Bayfield, Wisconsin, to Punta Gorda, Florida. In her book, *Adventures of a Once Reluctant Sailor: a Journey of Guts, Growth, and Grace*, she tells a delightful story of her inner thoughts and emotions as she sails with her husband, Wayne. She invites the reader to share their experience and follow along on the adventure. Fledgling sailors will learn about the art of sailing as Wayne, an experienced skipper, answers questions from readers of their blog. Michele writes, with humor and newly learned knowledge, on such things as preparing food on a moving vessel, keeping a lonely watch on a stormy night, and the importance of family and faith. She is a true inspiration to anyone who has ever wondered, 'Can I do it?'"

~ *Marilyn Thorndycraft, Punta Gorda, Florida*

"*Adventures of a Once Reluctant Sailor: a Journey of Guts, Growth, and Grace* is an entertaining and informative book for the experienced boater as well as armchair sailors and anyone contemplating their own nautical adventure on North America's inland and coastal waterways. I highly recommend it."

~ *Richard Lynch, Honolulu, Hawaii*

"In her book, *Adventures of a Once Reluctant Sailor: a Journey of Guts, Growth, and Grace,* Michele Sharp recounts a wonderful adventure. I enjoyed Michele's subtle humor and conversational style as she described their adventures and misadventures, both on the water and on land, and I looked forward with great anticipation to each new port of call. As a novice sailor, the book gave me great insight into the complexities as well as the mental and physical requirements of such a journey.

~ Dan Fradin, Plymouth, Minnesota

"Even though I followed the blog during their journey and knew the outcome of their adventure, I still could not put this book down and couldn't wait to see what happened next."

~ Sharon McClintock, Winter Haven, Florida

Adventures
of a
Once Reluctant
Sailor

A Journey of Guts, Growth, and Grace

Michele McClintock Sharp

To my dear friend
of 45 years - Marcia

Love,
Shelly
aka Michele Sharp

First Edition Printed, 2012

ISBN: 978-1-61005-231-3

Library of Congress Control Number: 2012913215

Printed in the United States of America by: BookLogix, Alpharetta, GA.

This paper meets the requirements of ANSI/NISO Z39.48-1992
   (Permanence of Paper)

This book may be purchased in bulk for educational, business, fundraising
   or sales promotional use. For information please contact:
   **Michele McClintock Sharp, www.reluctantsailor.net
   reluctantsailor@me.com**

Cover and interior layout design by: Vanessa Lowry

All photos were taken by Michele Sharp, except for the following:
   Photos of Michele were taken by Wayne Sharp
   Page 62 photo by Rachael Newman
   Page 201 photo by Norma Cavanaugh
   Photos of Wayne and Michele on pages 3, 50, 56 and 193 were
   taken by random strangers.

All maps © 2012 Google

Dedication

This book is dedicated to Wayne—my husband, sailboat captain, and contributor to the original blog, which was the foundation for this book.

It's a cliché: How many times have you read in a book's dedication or acknowledgements, "Thank you to so-and-so, without whom this book could not have been written?" Well, I'm here to perpetuate that cliché, because without Wayne, there would have been no sailing journey to write about. His contributions to the blog as he answered readers' questions were filled with wisdom, expertise, and technical knowledge that I lacked. During the trip, Wayne kept a detailed log of practical details, such as where we stayed and how far we traveled, which helped me fill in many blanks. He painstakingly provided the maps, wrote the Appendix with information about *Lena Bea*, and was my sounding board. Finally, Wayne's love, support, encouragement, and patience smoothed the way for me to write.

*The sea, once it
casts its spell,
holds one in its
net of wonder forever.*

~ *Jacques Yves Cousteau*

Table of Contents

Twenty years from now you will be more disappointed by the things you didn't do than by the ones you did do. So throw off the bowlines, sail away from the safe harbor. Catch the trade winds in your sails. Explore. Dream. Discover.

~ *Attributed to Mark Twain*

Foreword

In the 1970s, Michele traveled to Europe on three separate occasions. Her combined trips totaled nearly fifteen months and she visited eighteen countries. Sometime later I asked her if she would be willing to write about her experiences: the challenges, frustrations, the special moments, the lonely times, anything. She readily said yes but also asked why. I answered, "I believe what you write will help parents and their college age kids when the kids want to travel as you did and the parents declare 'Not in this lifetime' or something like that."

Michele wrote and wrote and wrote with a pen on notebook paper—some twenty-pages of memories, experiences and reflections. I long ago lost track of how many times I shared her writing with parents and their college age kids. I do know that Michele's honesty laced with humor in describing the people, places, customs she experienced, and the jobs she held, along with the occasional "did-I-really-do-that" events, moved many parents to give their blessings to similar adventures for their college kids.

Now, nearly forty years later, Michele captivates the reader with *Adventures of a Once Reluctant Sailor: a Journey of Guts, Growth, and Grace.* Michele fills each page with wit, wisdom and wonder. She acknowledges a touch of trepidation: how does Wayne's and her marriage—strong as it is—adapt to the constant togetherness and unique challenges of a 5,000 miles, months-long adventure on the *Lena Bea* as they sail the Great Lakes, the St. Lawrence Seaway and down the Atlantic Ocean and into the Gulf of Mexico to the dock in the back-yard of their home in Punta Gorda, FL. Her vivid use of words creates amazing pictures in the reader's mind as she describes encounters with huge freighters and even more massive air craft carriers. She tells of watching whales frolic and dolphins play. She relates the wonder found in solitude late at night as she sat at the helm. No land or other water craft in sight. The sky filled with stars. Michele sees anew the wonder of God's creative power. There are tales of consternation and change of plans, altering departure times, visits to emergency rooms, meeting people who become lifelong friends. Captain Wayne adds his voice and perspective from time to time. We smile as Wayne and Michele give us an amazing glimpse into their husband-wife adventure as Captain and First Mate.

Along the way, Michele invited readers of her blog to ask questions, even those burning questions we all want to ask but . . . decorum leads us not to. But someone does and the Captain or the First Mate answers. The questions range from specific details concerning the *Lena Bea* to what are the challenges of showering in a confined space that is constantly moving to how your faith influenced your journey. The questions intrigue; the answers inform and sometimes trigger a chuckle.

Adventures of a Once Reluctant Sailor: a Journey of Guts, Growth, and Grace is a page turner; not because it is filled with mystery and suspense, but because of the power of Michele's words which draw us into the journey and fill us with a passion to read one more page, learn of one more adventure.

Sit down in your favorite place to read. Set aside a good amount of time. You won't want to read Michele's book in short bites—although you could. Savor the word pictures that Michele crafts. Enhance those images with the photographs Michele took and has included in the book. Laugh. Wince at moments of misfortune. Celebrate the grace. Above all enjoy. And just maybe this record of *Adventures of a Once Reluctant Sailor: a Journey of Guts, Growth, and Grace* will move you to tackle your personal journey of guts, growth and grace.

Tim Morrison, President and Writing Coach,
Write Choice Services, Inc.,
Host of Business Radio X's Write Here, Write Now

*A ship in harbor is
safe—but that is not
what ships are built for.*

~ John A. Shedd

Acknowledgements

We have the most loving and supportive family. I'm not sure what they *really* thought when we told them of our plans for this trip, but if they had doubts or concerns, they mostly kept it to themselves.

Because contact with other people was limited, we reveled in every visit with friends and family along the way. To our kids: As you know, it was our greatest desire for you to visit us during our journey. Michael and Suzanne, you'll never know how much it meant to us that you did, and a big "thank you" to Amy and Brian for helping make it possible. Joe, you weren't able to meet up with us, but we appreciated your support, and your knowledge of Photoshop saved me while working on photos for the book.

Several people welcomed us into their homes for a refreshing break of "normal life" on land: Diane and John Raffo, thank you for your hospitality, for driving us around to do errands, and for meeting us in Rockport, Massachusetts. We *so* enjoyed the camaraderie. Diane and Terry Haglund and Karen Schwabe, thank you for the warm welcome and for so graciously offering us the use of your car. It was a delight to meet your families and reconnect after so many years.

Cousins Dave, Mary, and Jacob Decker met us in Cape Cod with their friend, Meg. My mom Sharon McClintock and her friend Mary Hannula met us in Charleston. In Annapolis we had the pleasure of meeting with two couples: First, Hayden and Raydeen Cochran, a couple Wayne knew from the Island Packet email list, who shared with us helpful information about sailing the Chesapeake. We also met with a business associate of Wayne's for over 25 years, Dan Interlandi and his wife Barbara, and enjoyed catching up with them. We thank you all for making the time and effort; it was such a treat! Many others wanted to meet up and we were sorry we couldn't work it out to be in the right places at the right times; it was truly our loss.

To other people we traveled with: Claus and Rachael Newman, I felt the thrills all over again as I relived our whale adventures while writing this book. There aren't many experiences in my life that have topped that one and having you to share it with made it so much richer. Gary DeSantis, we miss you so much and will always cherish the memories of your ten days sailing with us. Rest in peace, dear friend.

I am so grateful to those who read the manuscript for *Adventures of a Once Reluctant Sailor: a Journey of Guts, Growth, and Grace* and provided constructive feedback: Dan Fradin, Richard Lynch, Diana Maloney, Sharon McClintock, Tim Morrison, Marilyn Thorndycraft, and Jodi Wurzinger. I know how cumbersome it was to read the manuscript on your computer and appreciate your willingness to do it anyway. I took all of your suggestions to heart and made important changes based on some of your comments. Nancy Seamon-Krauss, Kim Halberg, Diana Maloney, Stacy Monson, Jon Shattuck, and Marilyn Thorndycraft—your wisdom, experience, and encouragement as fellow writers gave me an edge and a valuable perspective I wouldn't have had otherwise. Thank you.

Vanessa Lowry, owner of Connect 4 Leverage, is my graphic designer and couldn't be more delightful to work with. I have to confess that I felt a surprising level of anxiety as I turned "my baby" over to you, Vanessa, but you quickly earned my trust and put that anxiety to rest. Thank you for the beautiful cover design and interior formatting. Working with so many photos made this project more complicated than most, and your amazing design of the book makes me look much more professional than I feel.

Dr. Tim Morrison, President and Writing Coach of Write Choice Services, Inc. is my editor and mentor, but more importantly, my friend of more than forty years. Thank you, Tim, for gently prodding me to change what was necessary to make a successful transition from blog to book. I knew in my heart you were right, but that didn't make it easy to let go. The process was far more involved than I expected and I am grateful to you for your honesty, objectivity, counsel, support, and patience, but most of all, your friendship.

To readers of the blog who encouraged me and posted your questions and comments, I owe you a debt of gratitude—I didn't expect the blog to be so interactive, but that quality became a great incentive to keep it going. Without the reward of hearing back from you regularly (especially Tracy Decker, Karen Eno, and Paula Good), I may not have persevered with the blog to the end of the trip, and without the blog I would not remember enough about our trip to write a book about it. You were not only my lifeline on what otherwise would have been a very lonely trip, but a huge part of my inspiration. Several of you suggested early on that I write a book about our experiences, and you were front and center on my mind as I wrote *Adventures of a Once Reluctant Sailor: a Journey of Guts, Growth, and Grace.*

I went through the blog and made a list of all who contributed comments and questions, with the intention of including it here. However, there were other people who tried to post comments and weren't successful (Blogger can be "quirky"), and many sent emails (which I no longer have) instead. So I decided to acknowledge by name only those people I actually quoted in the book (the rest of you know who you are): Bill Boettner, Mary Decker, Tracy Decker, Gary DeSantis, Paula Good, Donna Lander, Melissa Larson, Tim Morrison, Claus and Rachael Newman, Robin Pool, Mike Sayler, Heidi Strommen, Alex Weimer, and Suzanne Weimer. My heartfelt thanks to you all!

Finally, I have to thank my mom, Sharon McClintock. Thank you, Mom, for sharing your perspective with my readers—I know many of them will be able to relate to what you were feeling. But more than that, thank you for your unwavering support and encouragement (well, it did waver a bit when I intentionally swam with the sharks while sailing in the Bahamas in '09). You never allowed your fears as a mother to hold me back from realizing my dreams—even as you sent me on my way to Europe for the first time when I was twenty, with a backpack, a friend, and no plan—so it never occurred to me to allow my own fears to hold me back. I am blessed to have you as my mom and I love you so much.

Introduction

We were sailing all night, 27½ hours straight, for 171 nautical miles. I had the first watch, all alone in the cockpit from 9:00 in the evening until 1:30 a.m.—in a thunderstorm! I'm sitting in this vessel, miles from land, the only object above water level as far as the eye can see. And in the midst of the storm, I am keenly aware of the mast—a 63-foot metal rod—sticking up from the middle of the boat, right above me! How's that for an invitation to a lightning bolt? And I'm wondering, *How did I get here, a landlubber from Minnesota, who is definitely not a sailor!* Well, in this book I'm going to explain how and why I got there. I hope you enjoy reading about my adventure as much I did living it.

~ ~ ~

I was not going to do this trip—it was waaayy outside my comfort zone.

Wayne had often expressed his wish to take a long sailing trip. Furthermore, his dream was to spend our winters living on the boat (our 37-foot Island Packet sailboat, *Wind Dancer*). I vetoed the idea because I had never known anyone who lived on a boat . . . Indeed, the whole *concept* of living on a boat was new to me—I'm from Minnesota, about the farthest point from the coast of any state in the U.S.—and it seemed like such a radical idea. Besides that, *Wind Dancer* lacked modern conveniences and equipment that I felt were necessary, I didn't think it was big enough (for me) to live in, and just the *thought* of confinement in such a small space nearly gave me claustrophobia. Also, I did not care to sail nearly as much as Wayne did. My dream was a condo with a dock for *Wind Dancer* in the backyard—the best of both worlds.

With the purchase of our Florida home (house, not condo) in February 2004, Wayne suddenly had a purpose and a destination for that long sailing trip. I agreed that we needed to get *Wind Dancer* down to Florida, but had my own ideas on how to get her there. My first choice: truck it down. My second choice: take it down the Mississippi (in my naiveté, I thought we could make a straight shot to the Gulf of Mexico from Minneapolis). Wayne's first choice: the East Coast by way of the Erie Canal and Hudson River; Wayne's second choice: to the Gulf of Mexico by way of Chicago, the Mississippi, and the Tennessee-Tombigbee Waterway to Mobile, Alabama. Part of my reasoning was that, initially, retirement was not in the picture (Wayne wasn't even sure he ever wanted to retire) and I thought three or four months was far too long for Wayne to be away from the business. It seemed to me that expedience was the wiser, albeit less adventurous, way to go.

Obviously, we needed to hash out a compromise. So how did our compromise result in a trip that was approximately 1500 miles longer than the longest route we had considered? And how did I end up making a trip I wanted little or no part of less than a year earlier?

In the spring of 2006, a large, regional competitor approached Wayne about buying the business. Negotiations moved along quickly, and by the middle of the summer they had an agreement. With my blessing and encouragement, since he would now be retired, Wayne started making plans to sail the boat down the East Coast through the Erie Canal and Hudson River. I intended to meet up with him and do a week here or there, but mostly he would be accompanied by other friends and sailors, who were eagerly lining up for the trip.

I had many reasons for not wanting to do the whole trip:

1) **Fear:** The thought of being in open water with no land in sight terrified me, as did the thought of being caught in a storm, and countless other Vague Unknowns.

2) **Inexperience:** The longest sailing trip I had ever done was a week; three or four months seemed like too much of a jump. I had no idea how I'd do on such a trip and was afraid I would be more of a liability than an asset to Wayne.

3) **Lack of interest:** Unlike Wayne, sailing is not my passion—to be honest, it was his thing and I went along with it.

4) **Homesickness and loneliness:** I just didn't want to be gone that long. I'm a homebody and like my land life too much and didn't want to be away from everyone for several months.

5) **Uncertainties with communication:** On previous sailing trips Wayne had been on in Lake Superior, cell phone service was almost nonexistent. I was concerned that we wouldn't be able to keep in contact with loved ones.

6) **Too much togetherness:** I am used to, and appreciate, having plenty of alone time, and frankly, the thought of being with someone—even my husband—24 hours a day, seven days a week, for three or four months made me very nervous.

Wayne closed on the business November 1 and, after much deliberation and research, bought *Lena Bea* about a month later from Gary DeSantis, who was a friend of Wayne's, the owner of Sailor's World Marina on Lake Minnetonka, and the regional Island Packet dealer.

Lena Bea (an Island Packet 445) was built the summer of 2005 and taken to Sailor's World in September, where she sat on a cradle at the marina for over a year. She had also been on display at the 2006 Minneapolis Boat Show. Frankly, she was more boat than we really needed, but Gary gave us such a good deal that nothing else made sense to us.

With the new, larger boat and its modern conveniences, like a microwave oven, large freezer and Vacu-Flush toilets (yes, I am spoiled), to say nothing of all the latest electronics, I began to consider the possibility of doing the entire trip. Only months away, the trip was becoming a reality and I was having second thoughts about missing out on the adventure. I reasoned that, if worse came to worst, Wayne could drop me off somewhere, I could fly home, and someone else could fly out to replace me.

Although he was leaning toward the Erie Canal/Hudson River route, Wayne still hadn't decided for certain. He continued to research his options.

Lena Bea was commissioned (put in the water for the first time and made operational with mast, rigging and sails) up in Bayfield, Wisconsin on Lake Superior on May 31, 2007, nearly two years after she was built and six months after we bought her. It was a major operation and the mast and stays alone weighed about 1500 pounds.

Both of the routes Wayne was considering would involve taking down the mast and rigging to pass under low bridges and putting it all back up again. When he saw the scope of what would be involved, he began to have second thoughts. "Stepping down" the mast is done routinely for boats that make the trip (you can hire people to do it for you), but most masts are ten or more feet shorter and much lighter than ours.

There was one route, however, that didn't require stepping down the mast: the St. Lawrence River. It would have been Wayne's first choice, but he hadn't really considered it because it was 1500 miles longer than the Erie Canal/Hudson River route. After talking to other sailors and doing more research, Wayne began to see it as a more attractive option. He mentioned the possibility to me, and to his surprise (and mine), I was excited about taking the St. Lawrence because it meant more wilderness to travel through and more adventure. The possibility of seeing whales hadn't even crossed our minds at that point.

So less than two months before departure, we finally chose our route and tacked 1500 miles (and a First Mate) onto the voyage. Initially, we planned to set sail on August 1; with the change of itinerary we decided to move up our departure, but Wayne still had an enormous amount of work to do before *Lena Bea* was ready to go.

It all started with a blog . . .

We decided that the easiest way to communicate with friends and family en route would be to keep an internet blog (although back then we hardly knew what that was). It certainly seemed to be more efficient and less cumbersome than sending emails or making countless repetitive phone calls. Staying in touch with loved ones was vital to us, and for friends and family back home in Minnesota and Texas or scattered about the country, a way to ease their anxiety about us taking such a voyage. They didn't know anyone who'd ever done such a "crazy" thing. Indeed, many of them had never been on a boat that didn't require paddles, and certainly not a boat you could sleep and cook on.

Well, to my surprise, the blog quickly took on a life of its own and became far more than just a way to keep loved ones in the loop as we traveled. First, I was amazed at how many people were reading the blog—not just friends and family, but their friends and family as well—and how interactive it became. People encouraged us and cheered us on by sending emails and commenting in response to my posts. Keeping the blog helped alleviate loneliness and became my social life. It also became my obsession, my journal, my creative outlet, and yes, my lifeline. I developed a compulsion to write and couldn't believe I had so much to say.

As the trip progressed and our memories were already beginning to blur (Where did we . . .? When did we . . .? What was the name of . . .?), we realized how vital the blog was to us as a memoir of our journey.

The blog was, in many respects, the third person with us on this journey, so it was important to me to retain the integrity of the blog as I worked on the manuscript for this book.

~ ~ ~

A "nautical mile" is one minute of latitude or approximately 6076 feet (about 1/8 longer than the statute mile of 5280 feet).

A "knot" is a measure of speed equal to one nautical mile (6076 feet) per hour.

Chapter 1

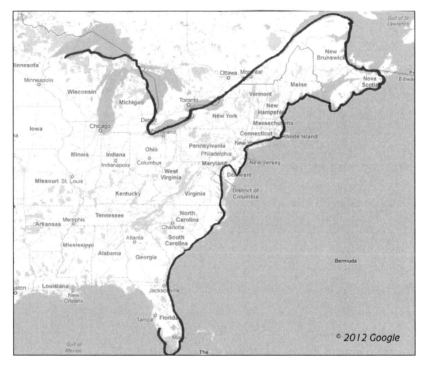

Preparing to
Get Underway

June 25 - July 27

*And the day came
when the risk to remain
tight in a bud was more
painful than the risk it
took to blossom.*

~ Anais Nin

Monday, June 25, 2007:

Ahoy!

Welcome to our blog, where Wayne and I will chronicle our sailing trip from Bayfield, Wisconsin to Punta Gorda, Florida aboard *Lena Bea*, a 2006 Island Packet 445. We bought her last November and Wayne has worked feverishly for months to prepare her for our journey. Our route of approximately 5000 miles will take us through the Great Lakes, the St. Lawrence River (including the cities of Montréal and Québec), New Brunswick, Prince Edward Island, Nova Scotia, across to Maine, down the Eastern Seaboard via the Atlantic Ocean and Intracoastal Waterway (ICW),  and around the Florida Keys north to Punta Gorda, where she will reside at the dock behind our home.

Our plan for this blog is to share the trip with friends and family back home. Of course, you can expect to see many photos of places we visit en route, so check back often.

Friday, July 20, 2007:

Looks like we're really going to do this!

As we scramble madly with final preparations, reality has hit: *We are really going to make this trip!* WOW! We've accomplished so much in such a short time. Preparations easily could have taken a year or more, especially considering Wayne had to install all the equipment, including the auto pilot, GPS, radar, VHF radio, two air conditioning and heating

systems, a generator, additional batteries, an inverter, and a feathering prop. He also installed a custom arch with davits for our dinghy and a place for mounting antennas, solar panels, and other equipment. Wayne did at least 95% of the work himself.

Our goal was to leave by today, but due to circumstances beyond our control—such as the delay of vital equipment—we had to postpone our departure until Tuesday, July 24. Experienced cruisers will tell you that a four-day delay is nothing; four weeks, four months, or even four years are more typical. Originally we had planned to leave the beginning of August, but when we decided at the end of May to take the St. Lawrence Seaway—an addition of approximately 1500 miles—the time factor became more critical and we decided to leave as soon as we could be ready. We want to allow plenty of time to enjoy the journey and stop along the way but still be headed south before the weather gets too cold. Because of those pesky hurricanes in the Atlantic, the insurance company requires us to stay north of 35 degrees latitude— around Cape Hatteras, North Carolina—until November 1. Hurricane season ends November 30. It will be a mad dash from there since we are expecting family to visit us in Punta Gorda the week of Thanksgiving.

After ten days at home, Wayne returned to Bayfield last night and is installing the rest of the electronics on *Lena Bea* while I wrap things up at home. He'll bring the car back on Sunday and Mom will drive us back up later that day (a four-hour drive from our home in Plymouth). We expect the final pieces to be delivered for installation on Monday, and if all goes smoothly, we will leave early Tuesday morning. Our first port of call will be Houghton, Michigan—a town familiar to us because that is where our older son Michael and his wife Amy went to college (at Michigan Tech).

Michael and Amy joined us the first time we had *Lena Bea* out on the water, the weekend of June 30; we were delighted with how well she sails. Good thing, huh?

The weekend of July 7 we had quite a boatful: Mom, our younger son Joey, my sister Bonnie, sister Ricki and her husband Scott, sister Andra and her son Justin, and sister Jodi and her son Brandon. We had the best time! The weather was perfect and we got in two beautiful afternoons of sailing, as well as a visit to Madeleine Island.

The weekend of July 13 we drove down to Columbia, Missouri, for one last granddaughter fix before our trip.

The visit with Alex and Suzanne was too short, but we made the most of the time we had. Our son-in-law Brian is enrolled in the National Academy at the FBI academy in Quantico, Virginia, for ten weeks. Spending the weekend with Papa Wayne and Gramichele was a good distraction for Alex, who is very lonesome for her daddy.

Friday, July 20, 2007:

Bad family news

Today my brother Brian learned that he has colon cancer. The doctor said it's curable and hasn't spread, but the tumor is large and blocking his colon. He requires surgery, obviously, but the doctor wants to do chemo and radiation to shrink the tumor first. Treatment will start on Monday.

In light of this, it doesn't feel good to be leaving right now. Please keep Brian in your thoughts and prayers.

Saturday, July 21, 2007:

Communication

We got a fantastic deal on a satellite phone with unlimited minutes and you are welcome to call us. I don't want to publish the phone number here on the internet, but we will email it to people. The service should be fairly dependable, but if you don't get through on the first try, wait five or ten minutes and try again . . . often there isn't a satellite close enough to get a signal. If we call you, the number will not show up on your caller ID; it will say something like "restricted," "out of area," or "unknown."

We'll have our cell phones too, of course, but won't always be in the range of cell towers. If you don't have our cell phone numbers, your call will be forwarded to my cell phone if you dial our home number in Plymouth, and you can always email us. We'll want to know what's happening with everyone and with things back home.

Communication is vital—I would not be making this trip if we couldn't contact or be contacted in case of an emergency.

~~~~~~

Wednesday, July 25, 2007:

Here I sit . . .

. . . on the boat at the marina (no, we have not yet left the dock), waiting for Wayne to finish working on the generator—an unplanned-for repair that's eaten up hours of precious time—so I can go down and get everything organized, which will probably take all day. Meanwhile, all I can do is look around at the mess and wonder what the heck I'm going to do with all this stuff! Trying to anticipate everything we could possibly need for the next four months and then trying to pare it all down to absolute essentials has been mind-boggling. Remember, we've never done a trip anything like this before. Sure, there will be stores along the way and we'll pick up provisions as we go, but we really don't know what to expect. I want to be well-prepared and don't want to buy stuff we already have at home, so we may as well take it with us if there's room.

7

Another challenge has been clothing: we need to pack for all kinds of weather as well as all sorts of activities (hiking, general sight-seeing, dinners out with friends along the way, maybe a show in New York). In the interest of time, I packed the clothes for both of us. Wayne will have a fit when he sees how much I brought, but hey, did I mention the laundry thing? I don't want to spend my time ashore sitting in a laundromat, and you can be sure that doing laundry is not even a blip on Wayne's radar.

I admit to a tendency to over-pack and over-prepare, especially when I'm anxious. And yes . . . I am a *tad* anxious.

So why haven't we left yet when we were supposed to have left Friday, Sunday, Tuesday? Boat stuff. Electronic stuff. And I-don't-know-what-all stuff. Maybe Wayne will fill you in later, if he ever reaches a point when there's nothing else to do but write about the trials and tribulations of commissioning a boat.

Mom came into town Sunday morning since we thought that would be the day she'd be driving us back up to Bayfield. We went to the hospital to visit Brian, then had lunch at Amy and Michael's with them and Amy's parents, who were in town visiting from Michigan. We also got together with Joey, our younger son. I talked to a frantic Wayne on Sunday afternoon and told him, "Hey, it's okay, no rush." Originally, Mom had a very small window of time when she could drive us up because she was expecting company this week, but because of Brian's illness and the possibility that he would be undergoing surgery this week, she cancelled her plans and her schedule was freed up.

Long story short: We finally got up here about 6:00 last night (Tuesday). The up side to the delay is that I finished doing everything at home that I needed to and more: made and froze two batches of soup, a batch of white chili, and two meatloaves (pre-sliced) for the trip, and cleaned the house from top to bottom (it's a great stress-reliever). Most of all, I had some quality time with Mom before the trip.

We had hoped to leave late today, anchor at Stockton Island for the night, and continue on to Houghton, Michigan, in the morning. An interesting coincidence (if you believe in coincidences): Another couple two boats over from us, Rachael and Claus, just happen to be making this same trip, only they plan to be gone fourteen months and will cut across to the Bahamas from somewhere around North Carolina. They intended to leave weeks ago and now we're neck and neck. I spoke to Rachael this morning and found out they have the same itinerary and plan to leave today as well, so I made them a friendly wager: whoever gets to Houghton last has the other couple over for drinks the first opportunity we have.

The vision of ice cold rum and Diet Cokes dissolved when I got back to the boat and heard Wayne mumble something about us being lucky if we're able to leave in a week.

Stay tuned . . .

Thursday, July 26, 2007:

Another day, another delay

After spending hours working on the generator thing on Wednesday, Wayne discovered a crack in the heat exchanger. He called Mas Power, who agreed to overnight us a new one. Well, Mas Power just called to inform us that they missed the UPS deadline yesterday, but will ship it today. Now we can't leave until tomorrow.

We did accomplish a lot yesterday, though, and I got most of our stuff stowed away. I'm in awe at the amount of storage space on this boat! I keep finding new places to stash stuff. Now if I can only remember where I put everything . . .

Claus and Rachael are—really!—leaving today, but have changed their route slightly. Instead of going through Houghton, Michigan, they are doing a straight shot to Sault Sainte Marie, Ontario, a trip of about 48 hours. We considered doing the same, but Claus and Rachael are both seasoned sailors and

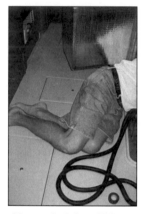

United States Coast Guard licensed boat captains (as is Wayne) with an experienced boat. Because *Lena Bea* is new and our crew—that would be me—a rookie, we decided to be prudent and take it easy at first.

Ironically, Wayne and I are feeling kind of relieved that we have an extra day to wrap things up. Wayne told me that because

Most typical view of Wayne

of some of the problems and delays he experienced, he discovered other problems that would have been more serious and harder to deal with after departure. We firmly believe that God's timing will be perfect and we will know when he is ready for us to leave.

Triumph over the generator

Romans 8:28 "And we know that in all things God works for the good of those who love him, who have been called according to his purpose."

~~~~~~

Friday, July 27, 2007:

Unplugged, stashed and ready to go

Yes, really. Just a quick post here, as we're scrambling to leave. When I tell people at the marina that today is the day, they just smile politely, nod, and give me a look that says, "Yeah, right—we'll believe it when you're gone, lady."

The new heat exchanger arrived today and Wayne installed it without a hitch. Meanwhile, I kept busy installing our Peek a Booo™ shutters. Now we have privacy—no more showering and changing clothes in the dark—and a way to keep out the sun. I also finished stashing everything. On a sailboat everything has to be put away and all cabinets and drawers latched, otherwise objects will go flying about the cabin, especially in heavy winds or rough water. Neither of those appears to be an issue tonight, though, because winds are calm and we'll probably have to motor all the way to Stockton Island.

An hour later and we are at the fuel dock to pump out our holding tank, fill our fresh water tank, and fuel the boat with diesel. I took some photos and will try to get them posted before we leave the dock and lose our internet connection.

Wayne's final task of the day will be to calibrate instruments—wind, speed, autopilot, and compass—on our way to Stockton Island.

Faith is taking the first step
even when you don't see the whole staircase.

~ *Martin Luther King, Jr.*

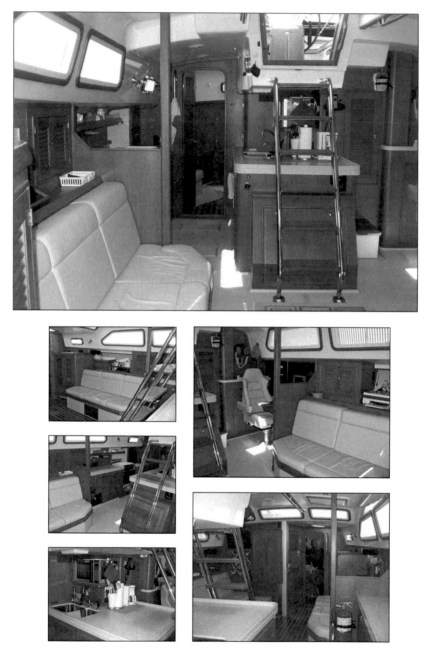

Our living quarters

Chapter 2

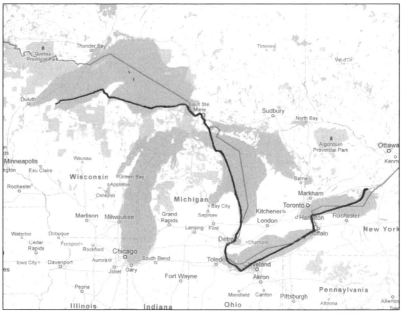

Lake Superior,
Lake Huron, Lake Erie,
and Lake Ontario

July 27 - August 8

*In almost everything that touches
our everyday life on earth, God
is pleased when we're pleased.
He wills that we be as free as
birds to soar and sing our
maker's praise without anxiety.*

~ A.W. Tozer

Friday, July 27, 2007:

Assimilation and reflection

It's our first night out and it couldn't be a more perfect and glorious send-off evening. I had dinner ready before Wayne dropped the anchor: lemon pepper chicken, salad, and a bottle of chardonnay. The lake is still and there's hardly a breeze. Stockton Island is a popular spot to anchor and camp, so I hear faint sounds of laughter, conversation, singing, recorded music, and the occasional splash of a fish breaking the surface of the water. I see the flicker of campfires and wafts of smoke from the island. I smell the subtle aroma of pine burning, a delicious blend of campfire and Christmas. Everything is tuned to just the right pitch, not so overpowering as to offend my senses. The moon is full and the sunset is so spectacular that I keep putting my computer down to grab my camera. This is what I like most about sailing. Thank you, God, for the bon voyage party! It's a good omen, don't you think? I envision God smiling and nodding his approval . . . for our timing and for trusting him enough to make this trip. I imagine his joy . . . at the adventure and personal growth that lie before us and the joy we will experience as we become intimate with his creation.

Random thoughts: I will miss the Apostle Islands. I will miss the town of Bayfield. I will miss the people at Port

Superior and Pike's Bay. Who knows if we will ever sail these waters again? I look out over the water and think, *We sure will be seeing a lot of this the next three months.* I wonder how my brother Brian is doing with his chemo and radiation treatments. I wonder if our Sea Bands will really keep us from getting seasick. I sure hope there's nothing to that nautical superstition about it being unlucky to embark on a Friday.

Wayne is down below calculating whether we need to leave at 3 or 4 a.m. to get to Houghton before the bridge closes tomorrow evening. With that thought, it's time to shut down the computer and get to bed.

First night out

First morning out

Saturday, July 28, 2007:

Approaching Houghton, Michigan

We awoke early and left our anchorage a little after 3:00 this morning. Sat in the cockpit in the dark, still half asleep, drinking our coffee mostly in silence. I went back to bed around 4:30. When I got up, I was astounded by the calmness of the water. This is Lake Superior? The lack of wind forced us to motor all day, but also gave us the chance to finish up some things around the boat.

Sunday, July 29, 2007:

Trolling for Wi-Fi

Yesterday we traveled about 105 nautical miles (or about 120 statute miles) at an average speed of seven knots, motoring for all but half an hour. It was a long day, having started shortly after 3 a.m., and we didn't anchor until 8 p.m. It will be another long one today; Wayne was up and going at about 3:15, I was up at 4:45. We have to stagger our sleep on these long passages so that one of us is always alert. Wayne is asleep right now and I'm on watch. Otto Pilot is driving, so I just check the instruments periodically to make sure there's nothing ominous on the radar and that we're still on course.

The instruments on this boat are amazing, but as with all things high tech, there is a learning curve. Wayne is in his glory playing around with them. Me? Well, I let him figure it all out and then show me what I need to know.

The coolest thing happened yesterday. We attempted to get Wi-Fi in Houghton, and although there were signals galore, we just couldn't connect to anything. Our main objective was to upload photos and order prints from Walgreens for Wayne's mom because she doesn't have a computer to follow our blog. After spending about half an hour anchored in Houghton trying to pick up a decent Wi-Fi signal, we finally gave up in frustration and continued on through Portage

Lake. I had our last two blog posts in my email outbox and decided, what the heck, I'll leave my computer running and hooked up to the Wi-Fi booster antenna and maybe I'll get lucky—sort of like throwing a hook in the water while you're boating to see if you catch any fish. Once anchored, I checked my email, and lo and behold, there were new messages and the posts had been sent! You can be sure we'll be "trolling for Wi-Fi" frequently. [At the time we did this trip, we, along with most people, were fairly naive about Wi-Fi. Today we would be far more concerned about security and careful about poaching bandwidth not intended for public consumption. Now people are far more likely to secure their networks.]

That works for email, and it's great that I can email posts to the blog, but getting online to upload photos, add links, or do anything else with the blog can't be done that way. I need an extended time online to fix up the blog and make it look more interesting. I'm new at this blog stuff and there's a lot to learn. I had never even *seen* a blog until about six months ago.

Fortunately, I have the blog set up to email me comments from others that are posted at the site. THANK YOU! to Tracy, Mary, Denise, and Alan for your comments! It's lonely out here and it's such a treat to hear from people. We also appreciate knowing that someone is actually reading our blog, so stop in and say hi when you get a chance, or just send an email. Do you have questions for us? If so, I'll answer them on the blog.

~~~~~

Monday, July 30, 2007:

Giving thanks and catching our breath

Psalm 147:1 "Praise the LORD. How good it is to sing praises to our God, how pleasant and fitting to praise him!"

Wayne and I are incredibly thankful for the ideal conditions God has blessed us with so far: perfect weather and blissfully calm water. True, with almost no wind we've sailed very little, but God granted us a few days to find our sea legs and acquaint ourselves with the new boat and equipment. This will sound strange, but it's been a blessing to not have the distraction and commotion of sailing; even Wayne agrees with that (well, somewhat). It's also been a treat to just veg out and relax after months of nonstop preparation activity. I like the calmness. We so appreciate the opportunity to sit and do nothing without long to-do lists hanging over our heads.

So, besides relaxing, how do we pass the time? Well, I work on the blog, obviously, and read our cruising guides to determine where to go and what to do when we get there. Besides the locations and amenities of marinas, the guides also show desirable anchorages and provide important information such as water depths and hazards. I've been taking photos and spend my free time sorting, editing, and preparing to upload them. Wayne continues to acquaint himself with the new instruments. Cell phone coverage has been surprisingly good, so we've been able to make some phone calls. Then there's just the day to day ordinary stuff, such as meal preparation and cleaning up.

We left our anchorage in Grand Marais, Michigan around 4:00 this morning. There was a little rain shower early, and Wayne had a visitor—a bat—join him in the cockpit. It was gone by the time I got up, but Wayne barricaded the companionway to keep the little guy out of the cabin and opened all the enclosure panels to facilitate his escape.

Half an hour ago we passed by Whitefish Point, where many of Lake Superior's shipwrecks are laid to rest. Wayne said there's a shipwreck museum there, which he visited when he did the Trans Superior Race in 2003. We're now headed for Sault Sainte Marie, Ontario, estimated time of arrival, 3:30-4:00 p.m. There will be internet access at the marina, and we will even get off of the boat and walk, go out for dinner, and go to the grocery store. After three days on the boat, I look forward to stretching my legs!

Tuesday, July 31, 2007:

Oh, Canada! You busted us at customs!

We're docked at Roberta Bondar Marina in Sault Sainte Marie. I am frantically trying to multitask online while watching the clock like a prisoner on death row: Reply to emails, upload photos, post to blog, download and install satellite data software, and if time allows, I'll read the news and get caught up on what's happening in the world. We need to leave by noon or so to get to our anchorage in the North Channel at a reasonable hour.

Yesterday we experienced the first of many locks, my first time ever. It was a bit nerve-wracking, especially not knowing what to expect, but all went smoothly.

After docking at the marina, our first duty was to check in with Canadian customs using a special phone on the dock. Wayne was up there for quite a while before he returned to the boat for an exact count of the alcoholic beverages on board. Now, we're not big drinkers, but probably over-provisioned in that department, too. We stocked up for the entire trip and brought extra wine and beer for guests. Frankly, a limit on alcohol and needing to pay duty on anything over that hadn't crossed our minds. Wayne returned to the customs phone, where I'm sure he told them—to the ounce—exactly how much we had. He disappeared into the marina office and was gone for a long time. I'm thinking, *Oh dear, they threw him in the slammer. Now who's going to drive this boat?* But no, they just taxed us $17 for our excess libations.

We grabbed a bite to eat at the restaurant next door, returned to the marina, and got online for a little while before turning in for a FULL night's sleep. It is sweltering hot here, so we were grateful to be plugged in at the dock and able to run our air conditioner without using the generator.

After today, I don't know when I'll be able to post again, unless Wayne can get our satellite data going; he's working on it.

Wednesday, August 1, 2007:

Down south, eh?

Okay, I just want to share a little trivia with you, eh. Of the following cities, which one is NOT referred to as "down south?" a) New Orleans, b) Atlanta, c) Toronto, d) Charleston, or e) none of the above? *You will find the answer at the bottom of this post.

We got away from "the Soo" later than planned this afternoon, about 2:40 p.m. Wayne hired Diesel Dave to come over and change the oil. He also repaired our bimini frame, which was damaged when Wayne accidentally lowered the boom on it (hmm, I wonder if that's where the expression came from) while trying out the electric winch. There wasn't a hose at the dock for filling our water tank and we hadn't thought to bring one, so Wayne ran over to Sears to pick one up. Sears didn't have the right kind of hose, but Roberta offered to drive Wayne to an RV place that sells them when she got off work at Sears at 1:30. Mission accomplished and we were finally on our way. Thank you, Roberta!

Tonight we will anchor in Milford Haven, on the west side of the North Channel. It was a recommendation from Fred, who was docked next to us. Fred was once chased by a bear!

In a little while we'll be passing a cargo ship named *Isolda.* She is en route to Duluth and will arrive on August 2 at 1 a.m. She's 657 feet long, has a 79 foot beam, and draws 19.7 feet. I could tell you a lot more about her if you were interested. How do I know all this? We have a cool electronic gadget called AIS (Automatic Identification System) that provides all kinds of information about other vessels it picks up on. I don't know too much about it, but will post a link with more information.

At this point, I must apologize to any mariners or techies out there for my limited nautical and technological knowledge and vocabulary. I am learning how to use the equipment (I *have* learned enough about the AIS to be able to look up the information on the ship myself), but understanding what the equipment does enough to explain it is another matter.

*The answer is e), none of the above. I learned from one of the dockhands that Canadians refer to Toronto as "down south." Who'd a thunk it?

Wednesday, August 1, 2007:

An early departure and sweet sailing

We left our anchorage in the North Channel at 6:00 this morning and have been sailing all day on a direct tack to Presque Isle, Michigan, our next anchorage. It has been glorious! Our intention was to spend two or three nights in the North Channel (it's a very popular cruising area), but last night I suddenly felt like it was time to move on. It turned out to be a good decision, because otherwise we would have been motoring and these lovely winds would have been wasted.

After years of sailing the sheltered waters of the Apostle Islands, it's really different to be sharing the waters with enormous freighters, up close and personal. We passed four yesterday, saw many others, and this morning one passed us up and cut across in front of us. Those ships leave a powerful wake!

A couple of days ago I suggested that people ask us questions, either by email or in the "comments" portion of each day's blog.

Here is our first QUESTION OF THE DAY: "How far apart are these places? For instance, if you run into bad weather, how far is it to the next rest stop? What determines your departure time?"

Answer: *We don't anticipate ever having to stop due to bad weather because Sirius marine weather service tells us what to expect before we leave every day. It gives us detailed information on winds, waves, barometric pressure, and so on, with sophisticated weather maps and storm warning alerts (I noticed there were tornado warnings in northern Florida a couple of days ago). If the weather looks ominous, we batten down the hatches (literally) and stay put. If it turns out to be seriously worse than expected, we will try to find a place to wait it out, but our Island Packet can handle any kind of weather. We, on the other hand, might be a bit uncomfortable.*

As far as distance between stops, that varies tremendously based on how fast we're able to travel on a given day. We've only been gone a short time, but Wayne says a reasonable estimate would probably be fifty to one hundred nautical miles a day.

We always have a destination in mind when we leave in the morning, and know the distance, what kind of winds we will likely have, approximately how much we will be able to sail versus motor, and about how long it will take us to get there. Currents will become a huge factor later on. We take all those factors into account to determine what time we need to leave in the morning to reach our destination by late afternoon.

Wednesday, August 1, 2007:

On the lam from U.S. customs

So we dock at Presque Isle Marina, and being good little Americans, call U.S. customs to let them know we're back in the country. The guy tells Wayne we need to go twenty miles in the opposite direction to check in. Yeah, right. Phooey on that, buddy, it isn't going to happen. Or to quote our painter, the colorful Mr. James Bailey, down in Florida: "Haaiil, no—we ain't doin' that!" We're on a *sailboat*, for crying out loud, and that would take all day. So I guess we're back in the U.S. illegally. Come and get us if you really care, Mr. Customs Official.

> QUESTION OF THE DAY: "Is there anything on the boat that you can do for exercise?"

Answer: *Well, we do have exercise DVDs and hand weights, and would even get some exercise, if only we'd use them. I keep telling myself that we're still trying to get into a routine, then I'll think about exercise. We also expect to walk a lot.*

Thursday, August 2, 2007:

Tranquility, tragedy, trials and triumph

4:30 a.m. We're sailing along at 6-7 knots, savoring a breakfast of hot oatmeal with dried cranberries, flax seed, cinnamon, and brown sugar, listening to jazz on NPR, watching the moon's reflection on the water. Life is good.

But then we remember and reality shatters our tiny bubble of bliss: the collapse of the 35W bridge in Minneapolis.

Our son Joey called and my cousin Denise emailed us about it last night. I woke up at 1:45 and couldn't get back to sleep; after tossing and turning for half an hour, I finally got up. "Are you up?" Wayne asked from the bedroom. "Yes," I responded. "Let's get going." Might as well, we're not going back to sleep. We were on our way by 3 a.m.

I can't imagine the horror, the mayhem, the grief. It's happening in Minneapolis. *Home.* There could be people we know at the bottom of the Mississippi River right now, entombed in their cars! I just want to be at home with my eyes glued to the TV like everyone else. The news on NPR doesn't tell us anything we don't already know.

Psalm 46:1-2 "God is our refuge and strength, an ever-present help in trouble. Therefore we will not fear, though the earth give way and the mountains fall into the heart of the sea."

The morning continues. There are a couple of minor irritations (they're all minor after yesterday's news): the cockpit is covered with a gazillion minuscule winged insects. They're on the screens, on the canvas, on the cushions and every other surface. We sit on them, walk on them, and brush them off our faces. I have bug guts on my legs and scrape them off with a fingernail. *What the heck?* All I can say is that it's a good thing they don't bite or we'd be in Lake Huron right now.

Minor irritation #2: The generator isn't charging the batteries and Wayne can't figure out why. There was no need to run the generator until yesterday because we were motoring and the engine was charging the batteries. Now we've been sailing and need to rely on the generator to do it, but something is amiss. There are solar panels for charging the batteries, but Wayne hasn't connected them yet because the wires were too big to fit through where they needed to go. Well, one way or another the problem will and must be fixed. For those who don't know, the batteries are necessary for powering everything on the boat—vital things such as the navigation instruments and the refrigerator, for instance.

Tonight we're docked in Harbor Beach, Michigan. Wayne fixed the battery charger problem. Hallelujah! That man is a genius.

The urgency to leave the North Channel when we did has become more obvious: today severe thunderstorms and small craft warnings were predicted for the North Channel and northern part of Lake Huron. Instead of contending with bad weather, we relished a day of great sailing. Someone up there is truly looking out for us.

QUESTION OF THE DAY: "How did you come up with the name *Lena Bea?*"

Answer: *We named her after our maternal grandmothers: Wayne's grandma was Lena, and Bea was a nickname for my grandma. Our mothers weren't thrilled with the name—they both thought we should have named her* Wind Dancer II.

Saturday, August 4, 2007:

Needing a boat break

We've been cruising for a week now (covered about 650 nautical miles) and are settling into a routine, establishing a rhythm, developing a synergy. It feels right; Wayne and I are a good team—we both know what needs to be done and do it. Life is good.

Yesterday I was in kind of a blue funk, though, and just couldn't figure out why. We by-passed two little towns on the St. Clair River that I would have liked to have stopped at for the night, and instead anchored in mud and weeds just offshore of a party town on Lake St. Clair, north of Detroit. I don't know what time it was when all the power boats roared by and rocked us awake, but I have an ugly suspicion that it was shortly after last call.

It took Wayne half an hour to clean mud from the anchor this morning.

It dawned on me that I need a leisurely boat break. I like to walk, sightsee, browse through little shops, those sorts of things, and we've done virtually none of it. That's by choice, of course (although I really did want to stop yesterday); we're sacrificing stops now for more desirable destinations later on when there's more to see and do. Pacing ourselves is tricky. My tendency is to enjoy the present. Wayne is good about letting me call the shots, but keeps us on track by balancing my tendency with his own of looking ahead and driving hard when the situation calls for it. I do agree with him most of the time. Yeah, we're a pretty good team.

If you have suggestions of good places to stop along our route, we'd appreciate hearing about them. You can either add a comment at the end of this post or email us. Normally we'd go online to get such information, but that's obviously not possible most of the time.

QUESTION OF THE DAY: "What does it mean to motor? Is that acceptable for sailboats? Is it cheating?"

Answer: *Good question! We sail if possible. If there isn't enough wind to sail or if the wind is coming from the wrong direction (directly in front of or behind the boat), we will, with great reluctance on Wayne's part, leave the sails down and motor. Motoring with the sail(s) up is another option and gives us a little more oomph in light winds. Motor-sailing is also helpful while going into strong wind and waves, as it enables us to point higher into the wind and affords us greater stability. Is it cheating? Some purists would say it is, except when docking. When you're cruising, though, and need to reach a destination before nightfall, running the engine is sometimes necessary and can be a vital means of controlling the boat in a strong current.*

Wind power is free, naturally, so we save a considerable sum of money when we sail rather than motor.

Of course, it would usually be considered cheating to motor during a race. In 2003 when Wayne, our son, Michael, and a few other guys raced Wind Dancer *in the Trans Superior Race, the winds were mostly dead calm and they just had to wait it out and take maximum advantage of every wisp of breeze that came along. The race participants were allowed to run their engines on a very limited basis, but there was a severe time penalty for doing so and they had to decide whether it was worthwhile. When Wayne joined Bill on* Summer's Dream *for the Chicago to Mackinaw Island race, running the engine at all was strictly prohibited.*

THE QUESTIONER ALSO ASKED: "Is there much noise when you motor? Is it necessary to motor some every day? Does this help keep batteries charged?"

Answer: *Yes, motoring is noisy and we hate that. On good days, we only use the engine when docking the boat (we always take down the sails and turn on the engine before entering a marina to give us better control of the boat). Running the engine does keep the batteries charged, and if we've been sailing a lot, it's sometimes necessary to run the engine to charge them and keep the refrigerator and instruments running. If the batteries aren't seriously low, we will wait until we've stopped for the day and plug into AC at the dock. If anchored, we run the generator.*

Tonight and tomorrow should give me the break I need: we'll be docking at an island, Put-In Bay Marina on Lake Erie, which is supposed to be an interesting place to stop. Better than that, though, is our destination on Sunday—our friends John and Diane's home in Vermilion, Ohio, where they have a dock waiting for us.

Sunday, August 5, 2007:

Sailing in the rain

Put-In Bay was one wild and crazy little town! Many bars, restaurants, T-shirt shops, and people. *And boats!* I've never seen so many boats packed so tightly into a place before; it looked like a tailgate party at a crowded used car dealership. Boats were rafted together at the docks with coolers stacked on the transoms and people wandered from boat to boat. Everyone appeared to be under (most of them *way* under) the age of 35 and there for one purpose: to party. Then there was us: we're way *over* the age of 35 and were back at the boat by 7:30. But that's okay. We were still able to hear the music from the boat . . . until very, very late. Little did we realize at the time how fortunate it was that they didn't have room for us at the dock or moorings—we could have ended up in the middle of a huge party regardless of our preference. Instead, we anchored a fair distance away, but not so far that we didn't feel a part of the action.

On our way to John and Diane's and it's been raining all morning, the first rain we've had since the start of our trip, except for a brief, light shower as we slept one night.

QUESTION OF THE DAY: "How do you get out and about when you are anchored? Taxi? Rental bikes?"

Answer: *Fortunately, we like to walk a lot, but will probably employ many forms of transportation before the end of this trip. Most people who cruise have a dinghy with a motor and use it to get to shore when anchored. Last night at Put-In-Bay, we opted to take a water taxi in to shore instead, though, and could have rented a golf cart, bikes, or mopeds to zip around the island, but it felt good to walk. Besides, walking was faster the streets were jammed with golf carts lined up bumper to bumper. Many cruisers travel with small, foldable bicycles.*

Monday, August 6, 2007:

Delightful time with John and Diane

We're enjoying a wonderful boat break while docked at John and Diane's house behind their sailboat, *Glory*, and have

been here since about 2:00 Sunday afternoon. John and Diane are such gracious hosts! They offered us their guest room, which we declined (Didn't want to get spoiled!), chauffeured us around to do errands, served us delicious meals, and John helped Wayne with projects on the boat. It was just great to be with friends! They live at the end of a lagoon lined with charming houses and flowers everywhere, and

their yard and home are beautiful. Since John and Diane are sailors, there has been plenty of sailing conversation.

Our plan is to leave midmorning tomorrow and sail straight through Lake Erie, nonstop to the Welland Canal, arriving sometime Wednesday afternoon.

Tuesday, August 7, 2007:

Waiting out a thunderstorm

Here we sit, still docked at John and Diane's, waiting out a thunderstorm. It appears we will be traveling in rain quite a bit the next couple of days.

Several people have said to me, "I should get a map so I can see where you are." I try to provide a hyperlink to a Google map for each location. The name of the town or whatever will be highlighted, so you can just click on it to bring up a Google map. From there you can zoom in or out for a better perspective.

I'd really like to upload more photos but need a large block of time online to do so. Sometimes you'll see our recent post with text only; I edit the text, upload the photos, and add hyperlinks when I can get online.

QUESTION OF THE DAY: "Michele, early on you referred to yourself as the 'first mate.' What is a first mate and what does he/she do?"

Answer: *A dictionary defines the first mate as the person on a boat that is second in charge after the captain and gives orders when the captain is busy. Obviously, the term is usually not used on a vessel with only two people, but I took the liberty of giving myself an Important Title, and I am the captain's mate, after all. So what does THIS first mate do since she has no one to give orders to?* Whatever the captain asks. *(Hmmm . . . What was I thinking? Maybe I should change my title to admiral—"commanding officer, ranking* above *the level of captain.")*

*A mind that is stretched
by new experiences can never go back
to its old dimensions.*

~ *Oliver Wendell Holmes Sr.*

Wednesday, August 8, 2007:

A long passage to Port Colborne, Ontario

It's been a long and exhausting two days, so don't expect anything witty, profound, or articulate here.

We finally left John and Diane's yesterday around noon during a break in the weather and sailed all night—wing-on-wing with the whisker pole, because the wind was directly behind us—until this afternoon at 3:30 (that's 27½ hours straight and 171 nautical miles). Wayne and I took turns on watch while the other slept; I took the first shift from about 9 p.m. until 1:30 a.m. There were some nasty thunderstorms, but they didn't last long, thank goodness! Call me crazy, but the words "sitting duck" kept coming to mind. You're sitting in this vessel in the water, the only object above the water level as far as the naked eye can see. Then you have this 63-foot metal rod sticking up from the middle of the vessel. Now, if I were a lightning bolt, I'd interpret that as an invitation. Might as well put a big target on us with the words "strike here." Of course, Wayne has a good explanation for how an Island Packet is constructed to minimize the effect of a lightning strike. Whatever.

There was some unwelcome excitement coming into Sugarloaf Marina in Port Colborne, Ontario today: high winds, strong currents, and difficulty docking.

We walked about a mile into town in search of an ATM today after learning that we will need $200 cash in Canadian dollars for the locks tomorrow (a $25 toll for each lock).

We have traveled over one thousand nautical miles since leaving home on July 27.

Put-In Bay

Chapter 3

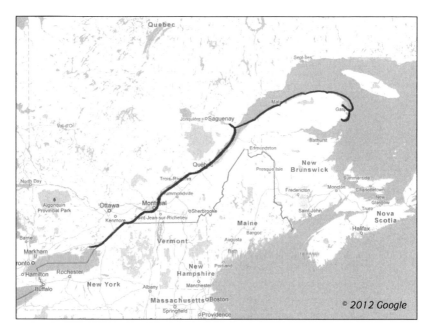

St. Lawrence River

August 9 - September 1

Fear is a self-imposed prison that will keep you from becoming what God intends for you to be.
You must move against it with the weapons of faith and love.

~ Rick Warren

Thursday, August 9, 2007:

Welland Canal

After a good night's sleep, we scrambled to get the boat ready for today's adventure: our trip through the Welland Canal. The Welland Canal connects Lake Ontario and Lake Erie through a series of eight locks, allowing ships that may be as much as 740 feet in length and thirty-thousand tons to travel between the two lakes in spite of the 326.5-foot difference in elevation (according to the Welland Canal website at www.wellandcanal.com/operation.htm). Crew requirements for passage on the Welland Canal are dependent on the direction of travel. Vessels going upward require a minimum of three crew members and vessels going downward require a minimum of two crew members. It takes an average of eleven hours to traverse the canal's length of 27 miles. We'll see how long it takes us.

Preparing the boat for the locks meant putting out extra fenders (including four straw ones we picked up yesterday for $20) to keep the boat away from the walls of the locks, and lines to maintain control of the boat. We had to secure everything on the boat, and gather anything we might need during the day—such as food and water—to keep close at hand in the cockpit. The voyage through the locks requires our constant presence and vigilance on deck; since we've never done this before and don't know what to expect, we've probably over-prepared, but better that than being caught unaware.

We got to our check-in point at 9:45 and were told it would probably be around noon before we could start. There were some freighters coming through, and since commercial vessels have priority, recreational traffic had to wait. That's fine. Unscheduled idle time around here is never idle and is usually an unexpected blessing. I finally did the dishes, which had been stacking up for a few days. I don't know if that qualifies as a blessing, but they're done.

In my haste and exhaustion last night, I didn't mention all the friendly and helpful people we met at Sugarloaf Marina, starting with a couple in a dinghy who gave us directions to our slip (yes, we needed the help). Next were the dockhand and some other boaters, who met us at the slip and kept us from seriously blowing into the dock. The Canadian customs officials met us at our boat and facilitated the process of customs. People kept stopping by to say hello and admire the boat. It's amazing how many people have connections to Punta Gorda and approach us when they see "Punta Gorda, Florida" on the transom—two different parties here. There was a boy about eleven or twelve years old who kept walking by and grinning at me, so I invited him aboard to see the boat. He was wide-eyed and awestruck. We met a young couple who hope to circumnavigate the world when their kids are grown. The kids working in the office went out of their way to accommodate us and even offered to drive us into town. On our way out of the marina this morning, people were waving and wishing us bon voyage. We'll have warm memories of our short stay in Port Colborne.

QUESTION OF THE DAY: "I assume the locks can only process one boat or ship at a time. Is it all first come first served, or do they take reservations?

Do they alternate upward- and downward-bound crafts? It seems amazing that they could keep up with the traffic."

Answer: *Well, I don't know the capacity, but they can process more than one at a time. We went through one lock with a large ship, and quite a few pleasure craft can go at a time. Freighters have priority, but it's first come first served for pleasure craft. Yes, upward and downward-bound crafts are alternated. I don't know if commercial vessels can make reservations or not, but recreational boats can't, so we just line up and wait. After the first lock, the rest of them know you're coming because the lock tenders (or whatever they're called) communicate with each other. Thankfully, there was very little traffic today; there are seven more locks to go through before Montréal, so we'll see what the next few days bring.*

Saturday, August 11, 2007:

Overnight crossing of Lake Ontario

We made it through the Welland Canal on Thursday, but it was a long, slow, and boring day—about eleven hours to get through the locks, much of it spent waiting.

Unfortunately, it was dark by the time we got through, which is never a good thing when you're trying to find a place to anchor or a dock to tie up to in a place you're unfamiliar with. We tried several times to radio the nearest marina, St. Catharine's, but they didn't respond. Since most of these marinas close by 8 p.m., there didn't seem to be much point in trying another one, but we were exhausted and needed a place to stay. Wayne carefully motored into St. Catharine's to see if there was a big enough slip nearby, but it was too dark to tell and too shallow to cruise around looking, so we made a U-turn and anchored in the bay to figure out our options. In my mind there was only one option: stay put and don't do anything until daylight. Who cares if the anchorage is only protected if winds aren't from the east but they are? Wayne was too tired to disagree, which is good, because I was too tired for a fight.

Note to selves: Call ahead if we'll be getting in late. Better yet, never arrive after dark if we don't have to.

Now we're in Lake Ontario, with a view of the New York shoreline on our right and the Toronto skyline on our left.

Tonight we have another overnight passage (across Lake Ontario) and will arrive at the mouth of the St. Lawrence River in the morning. I hope this overnighter is less exciting from a weather perspective than the last one.

I spent much of the day reading up on the Thousand Islands, St. Lawrence River, and Montréal.

Later . . . It's 12:15 a.m. and I am on watch while Wayne gets a few hours of sleep . . . or maybe I should say TRIES to get a few hours of sleep. I've had to wake him twice. The first time, I saw a 736-foot ship on radar, just on the other side of our waypoint and headed directly toward us. Novice that I am, I'm not about to make any navigational decisions, so Wayne got up and changed our course. I think I hit a wrong button or something a while later while making adjustments for the next waypoint, so I had to get him up again. He takes it all in stride.

So that's about all I do on watch—keep an eye on the radar, look around for other boats too small to show up on radar, and make sure Otto Pilot is keeping us on course. I make adjustments to the autopilot as necessary and wake Wayne when the situation calls for it. My constant attention isn't required, so I've also been reading and doing Sudoku puzzles. The concentration needed to do the puzzles helps keep me awake when I get drowsy reading, although that hasn't been a problem tonight. I have to be careful to keep the computer display and reading light dim, though, so they don't impair my night vision.

I want to thank you for reading our blog. It means so much to us that people care enough to follow our journey this way, in the midst of your busy lives. Blogging has turned out to be a really great way for us to communicate and we feel less lonely sharing the experience with you.

Later . . . It's 10:30 in the morning now. We anchored at 6:30 a.m. in Navy Bay in Kingston, Ontario where the St. Lawrence River begins. After a four-hour nap, we were ready to move on. Now we're ready for the day.

Sunday, August 12, 2007:

The Thousand Islands

Last night we anchored in the Thousand Islands, just off Thwartway Island. From here on, we plan to slow down, which is easier said than done when you've been like a perpetual motion machine—it's like trying to stop one of those 700-foot freighters. We'll be in Montréal before the weekend and will spend a couple of days there.

Our plan was to dock in Gananoque, Québec, just for the day and anchor again tonight. We need to do laundry, pick up some provisions and charts, study up on the locks, currents, and tides ahead of us, clean the boat, get online for a host of reasons, and I'd just like to wander around town and stretch my legs. There was no transient dockage available, though, so we had to dock for the night. The two main reasons we'd rather anchor are the peace and tranquility of anchoring and the expense of docking (about $65 here).

Swab the deck, Captain!

I'm sitting at a picnic table under a tree overlooking the marina while my laundry does its thing. Talk about sticker shock! Granted, it has been awhile since I've used a coin operated laundry facility— okay, nearly thirty years, back when all you needed were a few quarters—but jeepers! $2.00 a load to wash and $4.00 more if you want 'em dried! Canadian dollars, but still!

I am so envious of people who are cruising with their pets, and am surprised how many are. We lost Sophie, our West Highland Terrier, about fifteen months ago. It's only been recently that I've felt ready for another dog, but decided to wait until after this trip. That said, if someone came up to me with a dog or cat and asked if I'd like to take them, I don't think I would hesitate as long as the pet was agreeable to being on a boat (I hope Diana, a friend in Punta Gorda, didn't hear me say that or she will probably have one waiting for us on the dock when we get up in the morning).

Later . . . I finished my laundry and went to the grocery store. I walked for a couple of miles, and it felt *good*.

Oh, and note to selves: don't wait three weeks to do laundry. I should have taken Diane up on her offer to do it at their house.

Monday, August 13, 2007:

Gift or deprivation?

For weeks I've had an entry on my calendar, "Meteor shower dusk until dawn on the 13th, northeast horizon." We missed the peak shower time last night because of clouds and the lights in the marina, but now it's the evening of the 13th, the conditions are right, and I am ready.

August 13 is significant for another reason: Three years ago today, Hurricane Charley hit our home in Punta Gorda, causing us over $110,000 in damage and $13 billion statewide (we had just bought the house six months earlier). I muse over all that has happened since then and how, for many months afterward, we wondered if the repairs would ever be completed. When they were, though, we had an updated house with work done that needed to be done anyway.

We all have hurricanes in our lives and do finally recover from the vast majority of them, but in the meantime we wonder if we'll ever have a new roof over our heads or be finished picking up the pieces of the old one. We are never the same afterward, but hopefully wiser, stronger, with reorganized priorities and a greater focus on our Lord. He created us and only he has the blueprint to put us back together.

Isaiah 41:10 "So do not fear, for I am with you; do not be dismayed, for I am your God. I will strengthen you and help you; I will uphold you with my righteous right hand."

Now, where did all that come from?

The remarkable thing about my aforementioned calendar entry is that it's the only calendar entry I have since July 20, and except for an uncertain October entry of "Suz in Philly?"

and "Family in FL" the week of Thanksgiving, I have nothing else until a doctor appointment on December 17. Can you imagine that? Five months with no commitments? I can't really decide whether it's a gift or a deprivation; guess it could be either or both, depending on how you look at it.

If I could be granted one wish, it would be to have one of the kids join us for a week. Our son Michael wants to and is checking into where he might meet us. Wayne's daughter Suzanne has a conference in Philadelphia and could meet up with us, but hasn't decided if she will attend. Greg and Darlene, Wayne's brother and sister-in-law, are planning to go to New York in September to visit friends and family and, hopefully, sail with us a bit. Our niece Melanie is waiting in the wings, ready to meet us somewhere in September, and my sister Jodi would be delighted if we could meet up with her and her family in Cape Cod when they vacation there the end of this month. We would love to make it all work out, but here's the deal: you're moseying along at about six or seven knots, at the mercy of the weather, with no idea beyond the next week or so when you will be where. I have to say that's part of the beauty of this trip, the gift aspect, if you will, of five months with no commitments, no schedule: spontaneity. Having the freedom to stay here an extra day or two, or add a stop there, or take a side trip up this river. However, that does not mesh well with the need of others to plan ahead so they can join us . . . the deprivation aspect.

We'll try to work something out. Meanwhile, it's time to put this computer down and gaze at the heavens.

*You are never too old to set another goal
or to dream a new dream.*

~ *C.S. Lewis*

Monday, August 13, 2007:

A quiet evening at "home"

It's 5:30 p.m. and we're anchored off Grenadier Island on the north end of the Thousand Islands in the St. Lawrence River, about 130 nautical miles from Montréal; we should arrive on Thursday, depending on the locks. Yes, there are more locks ahead of us—seven between here and Montréal. I can hardly wait.

We heard a little while ago that Claus and Rachael (the couple from our marina) are in Montréal, so maybe we'll catch up with them in the next week or two. It would be fun to sit and swap war stories over dinner or drinks. I called and left a message for them.

We ate dinner early and have the rest of the evening to do whatever. It feels like a luxury. That sounds ironic, doesn't it?

When I was a child, I used to fantasize about living on my own island. It may have had something to do with being an introvert and living in a chaotic household with five siblings less than eight years younger than me, I don't know. Anyway, today I was utterly fascinated by all the single-dwelling islands we passed and went nuts photographing them.

Well, off to clean the bathrooms . . . lest you think we're getting away from it *all*.

Thousand Islands

Tuesday, August 14, 2007:

A nip in the air

Last night when we were getting ready for bed I commented to Wayne that it was the first day since leaving home that I didn't feel sticky with perspiration (he agreed, so it's not what you think). We slept with a comforter over us for the first time. This morning it was downright chilly and I threw on a pair of sweats . . . very quickly, I might add. We have been blessed with beautiful boating weather and very little rain, but would appreciate more wind for sailing.

We traveled sixty nautical miles in about 9-10 hours today and made it through three locks, which leaves us four tomorrow. We went with five other pleasure craft, rafted together in pairs or more with the larger vessel (that  would be us) next to the lock wall. Our waits were minimal, which is amazing since our book says the waits could be "as little as thirty minutes but not usually longer than four hours." Of course, we'll probably make up for it tomorrow.

Tonight we're anchored off the islands at St. Regis. This area is an Indian reservation and half the town of St. Regis is situated in New York and the other half in the Province of Québec.

Question of the day: "Michele, you've told us what you're doing to pass the time, but what about Wayne? What does he do at the end of the day?"

Answer: *Wayne does the major navigation stuff. Every night he records data in his captain's log for that day, plots our course for the next day, and checks weather. We have a*

Wi-Fi booster antenna, but only one of us can be plugged in at a time. Since we've agreed to make the blog a top priority, he doesn't get online much, even to check email. I am willing to

Gananoque, Quebec

give him a turn now and then, though, especially when it's time to pay the bills.

Friday, August 17, 2007:

Montréal

Just a quick update before we leave the dock in Montréal.

We made it through the remaining four locks (YAY!) and arrived at the marina in Montréal at 7:30 p.m. Our first task was to dispose of the bags of straw that served as additional fenders to protect the boat in the locks and help save wear and tear on the good fenders. They served their purpose, but we are happy they won't be needed again.

The energy of the city grabbed hold of me as the skyline grew, and I was nearly off the boat before we were in our slip. We ate dinner on the boat under the curious eyes of dozens of onlookers lined up on the wharf above us. Some people were even taking our picture! We finished hastily and went out to experience nightlife in Old Montréal. It was such a treat and

a much-needed change of scenery for us sensory-deprived mariners. Place Jacques Cartier, a popular pedestrian-only street in the heart of Old Montréal, is directly across from the marina. It's a vibrant place bordered on both sides with shops, restaurants, and cafes. The cobblestone streets and 17th and 18th century architecture give it a distinctly European flavor. Street artists, performers, and vendors add to the color and lively character of the area. What a delight it was to explore, observe, people-watch, and soak up the energy.

Thursday, besides more walking, we decided to make the most of a rainy day and our short time in Montréal by taking a bus tour—how very touristy of us—which

gave us a really fine overview of the city.

I was horrified and sad when the guide on our bus tour told us that some of the beautiful old cathedrals are being turned into apartments because "religion just isn't that popular anymore."

We were planning to spend a few days here, but another rainy day looms ahead tomorrow and Québec City awaits

us, so we decided to move on. Claus and Rachael are due to arrive there today, so we'll catch up with them Saturday evening or Sunday.

Québec City through Maine should be the highlight of our trip; I'm especially excited about Québec City to Nova Scotia—whale watching! You can be sure that my camera will be ready, with batteries fully charged and memory cards cleared.

Friday, August 17, 2007:

Adrenaline overdose

Fabulous sailing today, with winds that reached mid-20s at times. We flew the spinnaker for the first time and it was *awesome*. Well, except for the part when I was screaming with my eyes clamped shut, begging Wayne to call for a helicopter to come and get me. There were minor complications and the boat was heeled over so far the spinnaker was in the water. We sit quite high above the water in our center-cockpit boat, so that was more terrifying than you might expect.

The highlight of our day: Michael sent us an email to let us know he'll be joining us for a week in September! He'll fly to Charlottetown, Prince Edward Island, and will sail with us to Halifax, Nova Scotia. Of course we need to work out the timing, but as long as there are no big weather delays it should be fine. WOO-HOO! Doin' the happy dance!

Saturday, August 18, 2007:

Currents, tides, and a deflowered sailboat

I've gone back and edited some of my entries of the past few days and added photos and hyperlinks. I'm discovering that the words flow easier for me during the day because I'm not tired and rushed. I've also started to mention days of the week instead of "yesterday" or "tomorrow." This is to help me because we lose track of time, date, day of the week. I go back and look at some posts and don't remember for sure if they're in the correct order.

Navigating the St. Lawrence River is totally different from navigating the Great Lakes. In the Lakes you mostly just set your instruments to get you to your destination, keep an eye out for other boats, and keep on truckin'. In the St. Lawrence there are channels marked with red and green buoys that you must stay between or risk running aground. GPS in the river is less reliable because it can be off by as much as one hundred feet—a huge distance when you're trying to avoid shoals and underwater obstructions. We are amazed that there has been minimal commercial traffic on the St. Lawrence; we thought we'd be dodging freighters all the way down.

The current is working in our favor and now tides are becoming a factor as well; they bring currents of their own and can be a help or a hindrance, depending on whether the tide is coming in or going out. Wayne is "playing the tides," which means timing our travel so the tides work to our advantage. Where we stayed last night there is only about a foot-and-a-half rise and fall between low and high tide; in Québec City, only seventy miles farther downstream, the tidal range is eighteen feet! In a few miles we will pass through the Richelieu Rapids, a two-mile stretch of the river that can have a current of up to eight knots, which can make it difficult to control the boat.

Well, that was a nonevent. I just went up to ask Wayne how soon we'd be to the "rapids." He looked at the cruising guide and the charts and discovered they were behind us.

After Donnacona, just west of Québec City, the river widens considerably and enters the brackish water zone, the area where freshwater and saltwater meet. In this section, the salinity of the water rises from zero to twenty percent. So what, you may ask. Well, I'm here to tell you that this is where *Lena Bea* loses her virginity. Yep, that's right. Until now she has only been in relatively pristine fresh water. Now she will be subject to salt corrosion and other horrors.

In Lac St. Louis (a lake), before Montréal, Wayne had me take the helm for a while so he could put some things away. I carefully watched the buoys to make sure we stayed in the channel, but darned if I didn't get us off course (and in shallow water) by about a mile-and-a-half. I couldn't figure out how it happened until I read in our cruising guide later in the day that one needs to navigate carefully to avoid shallow areas, and that the buoys are confusing, which makes it a challenge to stay in the channel.

After visiting Montréal, a truly bilingual city, I was starting to think I might escape having to use my French while in Québec. Not so. Our stay last night in the small town marina of Trois-Rivières seemed devoid of anyone fluent in English, so we made do with my French. It worked fine except when Wayne asked if I could explain to the management that we didn't have electricity because of "reverse polarity." I could not have explained that in English, much less French.

It was so windy in Trois-Rivières that the channel markers were all blown to one side. Not knowing where the channel was, we had to ease our way slowly to find our way through and avoid running aground.

Wayne and I were talking about the trip and all the great places we are undoubtedly passing up. I commented that after the trip people will probably be asking us "Did you do this? Did you go there? Did you stop here?" There wasn't nearly enough time to do research and plan before we left, and our resources are limited now, so if you know of any "must see or do" places along the way that are sailboat accessible, we would be grateful for suggestions.

I originally started this blog as a lark, but it's become my obsession, my connection to you, my journal, my creative outlet, and yes, my lifeline. Thanks for accompanying us on our journey; I delight in sharing it with you.

Tuesday, August 21, 2007:

A joyful reunion in Québec City

After checking in at the Old Québec City Marina on Saturday evening, we went to find Claus and Rachael. What a joyful reunion that was! The conversation was animated and without pause for the couple of hours we spent with them and their cat, Charlotte, aboard *Kyanna*. Although we just met this summer because we "happened" to be docked two slips apart at Pike's Bay, it feels as if we've known each other much longer. Sharing a first adventure like this (although they've sailed more than we) at the same time will do that. It was fun to compare our experiences.

On Sunday morning we were invited to join Claus and Rachael on Bill and Nancy's boat, just a few over from ours. Bill and Nancy are acquaintances of Rachael's aunt and uncle in Park City, Utah, and old salts with endless stories to share. Bill counseled Wayne and Rachael (who took scrupulous notes) on the fine details of navigating the waters of the rest of the St. Lawrence, New Brunswick, Prince Edward Island, Nova Scotia, and Maine. They pored over the charts while Claus and I, who aren't navigators, followed along with our road maps. The other three would be talking about latitude and longitude, and Claus would say, "That's G5 on our map."

After lunch we went our separate ways but soon bumped into Claus and Rachael on antique row and continued our exploration of the Old City of Québec with them, Rachael with her Nikon D200 and me with my Nikon D80. The guys get credit for their patience, because our pace went something like "walk twenty feet, stop and take a picture" all through the Old City. Rachael and I rewarded Wayne and Claus with a beer stop later in the afternoon, and we finally

settled on dinner at a little French restaurant after checking out nearly every menu posted in the Old City. Too many enticing restaurants to choose from.

We like Québec even more than Montréal; it has more of the Old World charm and atmosphere and more buildings and sites of historical and architectural appeal. It is the last remaining fortified city north of Mexico City, which adds a unique element of interest. Québec City is said to be the only place in North America to have retained so much of its European heritage. Walking the cobbled streets within the walls of the old city, one has the unmistakable impression of being in Europe, except for the almost jarring disparity of seeing signs and shops with Canadian, Native American, and Inuit merchandise, arts, and souvenirs.

We returned to the boat late Sunday evening, but not too late to call and wish our granddaughter Alex a happy fifth birthday.

Monday morning there was another session with Bill and Nancy, covering the area from Maine down to the Chesapeake Bay. They're from Rhode Island and know the East Coast particularly well. They shared with us a treasure trove of information, and we are grateful to them for their generosity. Bill and Nancy are dear people who are young at heart and fun to be with. They spend their winters in Park City, Utah, where it is Bill's goal to become the oldest ski instructor there.

After lunch I felt the need to explore on my own and Wayne had work to do. I went to the farmer's market nearby. Oh, my! Wayne and I visited there on Sunday, too. I have never seen so much beautiful produce! Baskets of freshly picked berries, piles of sweet corn, gunny sacks full of potatoes, bundles of leeks, onions, carrots, and herbs, heads of broccoli and cauliflower, buckets full of flowers, every kind of squash imaginable, cheeses, teas, maple syrup, freshly baked bread . . . and all of it displayed so beautifully. It was a feast for the eyes and overwhelming to us fresh produce-deprived mariners.

I walked for over four hours and returned to the boat worn out and weighted down with goodies from the market. Wayne greeted me with "Let's go to the grocery store!" so we walked twenty minutes over there and picked up things not available at the market.

On the way back our four friends summoned us to join them for cocktails on Bill and Nancy's boat. We dropped off our groceries, heated up some spinach and artichoke dip from the freezer, and went on over. The six of us shared stories, laughed, and just delighted in the company of like-minded friends.

I invited Claus and Rachael over for dinner, with the thought that we could plot and discuss our course since we've decided to travel together for a while. I don't know how much plotting took place, but animated conversation and laughter certainly did.

Earlier in the day Claus said to me, "I'm feeling the itch," and I knew exactly what he was talking about: we love it here in Québec, but were feeling the urge to "hit the road." In spite of that, we decided to stay another day. We'll be cruising mostly in wilderness area for the next couple of weeks and want to be well-provisioned and prepared before we venture out. I did a couple loads of laundry, answered email, got some things organized, and am working on this blog. I hope to get photos uploaded this afternoon. Wayne has been—all together now—working on the boat, and I hope he'll have time to get a couple of things done on my honey-do list before the day's out. I have encouraged him to post to the blog, which he intends to do but hasn't gotten around to it yet.

Wednesday, August 22, 2007:

Leaving Québec City

Just a quick note here to let you know of our plans before we head over for fuel and a pump out.

Today we leave with Claus and Rachael and will travel sixty miles to anchor off Île Aux Coudres. Tomorrow we will travel to Tadoussac and from there, up the Saguenay River, a fjord. The mouth of the Saguenay is one of the best places in the world for whale-watching, and I can hardly wait!

I don't know when we will have internet access or if our cell phones will work, but we do have our satellite phone and will check in with family.

Thursday, August 23, 2007:

First whale sighting—BELUGAS!

Can you imagine looking out your kitchen window and seeing whales, just as you and I might see squirrels or deer?

Yet whales are a common sight on the St. Lawrence River, because

they are attracted by the river's abundant shellfish and its impressive depth, even close to shore in many places. The province of Québec is one of the few places in the world where you can see such a wide variety of whales—thirteen to fifteen different species!

Today we experienced our first whale sighting, and, surprisingly, it was a beluga! What a thrill that was!

We left Île Aux Coudres at 12:15 p.m. and *sailed* the entire 26 miles to Tadoussac . . . with our spinnaker (the big, colorful sail)! An added bonus was that Rachael—a very competent photographer—photographed us while we were underway. Coming in to Tadoussac, we saw Minke whales swimming just twenty feet from the boat. We picked up a mooring ball after trying unsuccessfully to get our anchor to hold.

August 24 – Left Tadoussac at 9 a.m. to motor 31 nautical miles up the Saguenay Fjord. This is an area of awesome beauty and tranquility. The fog and rain we traveled in all day made it feel dreamlike, and the sightings of a few whales,

dolphins, and seals enhanced the experience. We moored in Eternity Bay at 2:30 and stayed two nights.

photo by Rachael Newman

See the beluga?

Sunday, August 26, 2007:

Best birthday ever

Today is my birthday, and it was a memorable one.

I woke up in this fabulous boat, moored in Eternity Bay on the Saguenay Fjord, surrounded by a breathtaking mountain vista. The sun, which we hadn't seen since leaving Québec, was trying hard to make an appearance. Wayne and Claus made a dinghy run to shore with our garbage and met a family with four kids from Ottawa, who were finishing up a two-month sailing trip. They had been to some of the places we will visit in the coming weeks, so Claus invited them over to *Kyanna* to look over charts and give us suggestions. Coincidentally, one of the daughters was also celebrating her birthday.

We left around noon; it was a beautiful day and we sailed the spinnaker most of the way back to Tadoussac.

We moored near the marina in Tadoussac at 4 p.m. (a challenge under heavy winds) and took the dinghy to shore. What a charming town! We walked around, took photos, and went to the grocery store before returning to *Lena Bea* for hors d'oeuvres and then to *Kyanna* for dinner. A surprise awaited us when we returned to the dinghy  after our walk: the tide had gone out, leaving the dinghy sitting on the beach. We're new to this tide business, and it will take some getting used to.

Rachael served a delicious birthday dinner of pork chops, green beans, a fresh baguette, French Rabbit chardonnay, and for dessert, a flourless chocolate torte. Yum! They even had birthday presents for me. Claus and Rachael have become such dear friends in such a short time.

Before bed, I checked my email and found this one from my stepdaughter Suzanne and granddaughter Alex: "Happy Birthday to Gramichele! We are thinking of you. Alex says 'I love you and have a good, safe trip. I hope you are well and that you are having a fun weekend!' Love, Alex and Suzanne."

Yes, I am blessed.

Monday, August 27, 2007:

Whales, whales, and more whales

We are sitting in the cockpit sipping our morning coffee, preparing to start our day. The rising sun glistens on the water and whales blow in the harbor. A lone seal swims by occasionally and glances at us warily without changing course. "We get to do this!" as Claus would say. And our adventure today raised the bar on "this" to an all new level.

I've decided to skip all the superlatives, as none are adequate, and let the whale photos speak for themselves. The photos don't begin to do them justice either, because they don't capture the essence, experience, and emotions of being there. And because these whales don't jump out of the water (not that we've seen, anyway) and their bodies are mostly submerged, it's impossible to fully appreciate their massive size.

I found many internet sites with information on whales. Here are some facts I gleaned: The Blue Whale is the largest animal known to have ever lived on Earth. They can grow up to 100 feet long, weigh up to 200 tons, and eat four tons or more of food per day! They are protected and endangered; the St. Lawrence population is estimated at 60-100 and the entire North Atlantic population is probably less than 1000.

The beluga or white whale is also protected and endangered. Their numbers in the St. Lawrence are estimated at around 1000 and declining due to environmental toxins.

Heading out into the bay this morning we observed the commercial whale watching boats, and when they stopped and congregated, we knew to look for whales if they had not already made their presence known to us. We watched blue whales blowing and breaching, heard them breathing and moaning. Rachael and I stood in our bowsprits, cameras clicking wildly, while Wayne and Claus kept busy trying to aim the boats to where we pointed.

The blue whales had disappeared and we were sitting back, relishing the experience. All of a sudden the water surface seemed covered with whitecaps and my immediate thought was, *Belugas.* Then I laughed and thought to myself, *Now I'm imagining that every little thing is a whale.* Except they *were* belugas and we were *surrounded* by them . . . over 100 for sure.

They swam past the boat, swam up to the boat, swam under the boat, and I couldn't shoot my camera fast enough. Wayne put the engine in neutral, as we understood the protocol to be. We realized we were in a marine park sanctuary when the park patrol boat interrupted our experience and set us straight: If you find yourself in a pod of belugas, you are supposed to leave the area immediately and stay at least 400 meters away (200 meters from blue whales). While they kindly educated Wayne about whale etiquette, I kept taking photos, including some of *Kyanna* with Rachael taking photos of the belugas.

We saw other species of whales too, including minke and fin whales (according to Claus, who knows more about them than we do, which is absolutely nothing), and many seals as well. The seals don't photograph well; they just look like smooth black lumps in the water.

All day long the thought kept crossing my mind: this experience is beyond anything I had ever even dreamed of.

Dinner this evening with Claus and Rachael anchored off Île du Bic was a celebration of another kind. We bubbled with conversation about our shared experience, one of the most awesome of our lives. We had "show and tell," reliving the day while sharing our photos, oohing and ahhing as over a pile of precious gems.

~~~

Wednesday, August 29, 2007:

We're stick-in-the-muds

August 28 – We sailed the spinnaker again and docked at Marina Matane, having traveled 54 nautical miles. Rachael bought fresh scallops and shrimp and made a delicious seafood bisque for dinner. We expect to get our fill of seafood in the weeks ahead, and boy are we ready!

When you approach a marina, you call them on your VHF radio to tell them the size of your boat and your draft (how deep into the water it goes—ours is five feet) so the marina knows whether they can accommodate you. Normally they will then direct you to a slip. Today we tried several times to hail the marina, but didn't hear back from them, so we ventured in and docked ourselves. Well, after dinner we realized that the ebbing tide had left both of our boats sitting on the bottom of our slips. Thankfully, this is not a serious problem unless you're planning to leave before the flood tide, in which case you're stuck—literally. During the night I felt the boat begin to rock and knew the tide had come in; we had set our alarms so we could leave at 6:00, before it got too low again.

August 29 – It's around noon and we're about to dock at Marina Sainte-Anne-des-Monts, where I hope to have internet access so I can finally get these messages and photos posted. Calm seas provided us with good visibility this morning, so we saw dolphins, a few whales, and seals.

We're on the south shore of the St. Lawrence, still in Québec, but New Brunswick is just south of us.

QUESTION OF THE DAY: "Do you have TV and radio on board?"

Answer: *Technically, yes; we have a TV which is hooked up to an antenna (no satellite), but have had it on maybe twice since the start of the trip. Ironically, we either don't have time to watch it or need to conserve our batteries. For the most part, though, we forget it's there because we have never had a TV on a boat until this trip. I miss keeping up with world events and local news, but apart from that we hardly miss it.*

As far as the radio goes, we do have Sirius satellite radio but haven't been able to get it working yet. [We thought our Sirius weather subscription included radio, but later learned that Sirius radio required a separate subscription. Then we learned that a Raymarine software update was required to allow the Sirius radio to work, but it wasn't available until after the end of the trip.]

There is no Wi-Fi access at Marina Sainte-Anne-des-Monts and it seems the only place that has wireless is Pub Chez Bass. I asked Rachael if she wanted to go with me and she responded with a vehement "NO! That's a biker bar." She and Claus had walked past earlier and there were dozens of motorcycles parked outside. Oh, who cares? Dedicated blogger that I am, I was not going to let a few people on motorcycles keep me away. Wayne offered to escort me to the pub, which turned out to be totally unnecessary because all the bikers were gone by the time we got here. Wayne hung around long enough to consume a beer and an order of fish and chips before returning to the boat, but I'm supposed to call him on the two-way radio when I'm ready to leave (there is no cell phone service here) so he can walk me back. He is so chivalrous.

Thursday, August 30, 2007:

It's all south from here

August 30 – Today we reached the northernmost point on our journey, at 49.17.339 degrees latitude, about the same latitude as Winnipeg. That's a big turning point for the four of us—figuratively as well as literally. It seems appropriate that fog and chill (60ish) have been the order of the day. I think we're now in the Gulf of St. Lawrence, although my map does not tell me where the river ends and the Gulf begins. It just feels like the Gulf. One week from today we'll meet Michael in Charlottetown, Prince Edward Island. We are so looking forward to having him with us for a week!

We're anchored at Grande Vallée behind the public wharf. We hope to be within range of a cell phone tower later today or tomorrow.

Friday, August 31, 2007:

Another whale of a day

Wayne and I were ready to leave at 4 a.m. as agreed upon, but had to blow our air horn to rouse *Kyanna's* occupants.

We were cruising along in the fog, the gray of the sky merging seamlessly with the gray of the water. Only *Lena Bea* broke the dead calm of the sea and there was no other boat in sight, creating a perfect backdrop for what was to come.

Suddenly out of the stillness something black appeared—a whale!—breaching and spouting. And another . . . and another . . . and another. They were

everywhere, some so close to the boat (50 feet) that we could hear them breathe! I grabbed my camera and started

shooting, turning to where the sounds came from, wishing I had eyes on both sides of my head, four arms, and two cameras with which to capture it all. Wayne cut the engine and we watched in awe—just us and the whales—no tour boats and no marine park police to tell us to keep away. Were we afraid, knowing that some of these whales were possibly twice the size of our boat? It never crossed our minds.

1 Chronicles 29:11: "Yours, LORD, is the greatness and the power and the glory and the majesty and the splendor, for everything in heaven and earth is yours."

We finally, but reluctantly moved on. We radioed Claus and Rachael, who were a couple of miles behind us, to give them a heads up, excited to tell them about our whale encounter and hoping they would experience the same (which they did).

Spent the night tied up to the dock at Marina Gaspé.

Saturday, September 1, 2007:

Change of plans

September 1 – What is the saying? "We cannot change the winds, but we can adjust our sails." Something like that.

We intended today to be leisurely, having planned to cover a shorter distance and allowed time to hike, birdwatch, and take photos on Île Bonaventure, which has the largest colony of Northern Gannet in the world. The island has high cliffs with numerous ledges and fissures which make an ideal habitat for them and many other nesting seabirds. Well, it was not to be. The winds were too strong and the waves too rough to anchor, so plan B was to dock at Percé Village and take a tour boat to the island. Claus and Rachael were ahead of us scouting out our options. They thought the marina looked too small to safely maneuver and dock our boats in with the conditions we had, so we sailed past Percé Village, detoured slightly to photograph Percé Rock (quite impressive), continued on past the little harbor village, L'Anse-à-Beaufils, where we had planned to spend the night, and moved to plan

C. Claus and Rachael's next choice looked tenuous as well, so we went a little farther and docked at Grande Rivière. We knew immediately that this was a fishing village (besides the fact that our navigational chart labels the waters here as a "fish farm"), and would have even if we hadn't been surrounded by fishing boats—the aroma made it obvious.

We tied up and relaxed for a little while, then set out to explore the village. Well, we only made it as far as the fish market, just a stone's throw from the dock, because dinner was waiting for us inside—whole, live lobsters.

I made it clear that I would have nothing to do with torturing and murdering the poor things myself, so someone else would have to do it (yes, yes, I am a shameless hypocrite). On the walk back I realized that I did not even want *Lena Bea* to be the scene of the crime, so I asked Claus and Rachael if they would do the deed at their place while I prepared the rest of the dinner. Thankfully, they agreed.

Now, before I bought the lobsters I mentioned to Rachael that we didn't have any equipment for eating them and she

 assured me that they had some. Little did I know that Rachael's lobster-eating tools included wire cutters and an assortment of heavily used pairs of pliers. Of course, there was no way we would let the "wrong" equipment stop us from eating the lobster, though—sure, it took us a little longer, but the lobster was delish! Rust and all.

Tonight I proposed a toast in honor of it being our final night in Québec. We love Québec and the people are friendly, helpful, and gracious, but after a couple of weeks here, we look forward to the ease of being back in an English-speaking province.

Chapter 4

New Brunswick, Prince Edward Island, and Nova Scotia

September 2 - September 16

I learned that courage was not the absence of fear, but the triumph over it. The brave man is not he who does not feel afraid, but he who conquers that fear.

~ Nelson Mandela

Sunday, September 2, 2007:

Tongues and cheeks

September 2 – Tonight we are docked in Escuminac, New Brunswick. Along the way, especially in the small villages, people have been fascinated with our boats. Countless times we've been down in the cabin and looked up to see people on the dock checking out the boat or even peering in the windows. Often ours are the only sailboats, and in the last couple of places, ours have been practically the only non-fishing vessels in the marina. Tonight after dinner dad must have said to mom and the kids, "Hey, there are a couple of yachts in the marina; let's go check 'em out," because there was quite a parade of families on the dock.

Everyone we've met here has been so friendly. This afternoon we were chatting with a fisherman and asked about internet access; it wasn't available at the marina, but he invited us to come over to his house and use his internet service. A family strolled by and stopped to chat with us; they were visiting the dad's parents and pointed out the house, saying, "If you need anything, just come on over to the house."

Tonight we ate dinner aboard *Kyanna*. Besides trout, Rachael served us trout and cod tongues and cheeks— really!—which she bought at the same seafood market where we got the lobster. Well, it was unanimous: the cheeks were delicious (as was the trout)—think filet mignon. The tongues, well, not so much. In fact, they were awful. Even Charlotte the cat turned up his nose at them (yes, Charlotte is a boy).

One of the fishermen told us there hasn't been any cod this year, so what I'd like to know is, where the heck did all of those cod tongues and cheeks come from?

Monday, September 3, 2007:

Battered, beaten, and thoroughly stressed

September 3 – We left Escuminac at 7:10 a.m. and arrived in Bouctouche, New Brunswick, around 8:45 p.m., but covered only 75 nautical miles. What a day! We fought 20-30-knot winds head on and waves as high as eight feet under sunny skies. It felt as if the boat had become possessed by a herd of wild mustangs. The waves pounded us relentlessly and crashed over the bow, sometimes hitting the dodger (windshield) with what seemed to be the force of a fire hose. To make matters worse, we had to navigate our way around a minefield of lobster pot buoys—hundreds of them—and it would be a very bad thing to get one tangled in our propeller.

Our diligence in avoiding the buoys did not help us avoid engine problems, however. It overheated three times, and each time Wayne turned it off and went down below to investigate. The first time he added coolant, the second time he extracted seaweed from the filter, and the third time he discovered that the intake hose was totally clogged with seaweed. He managed to dig it out with a wire coat hanger (one of his favorite tools) bent into a hook on the end, but this whole process took a long time, and with each engine shutdown the wind blew us more off course.

Keep in mind that as Wayne worked, lying on his belly on the floor, the boat lurched, heeled, and catapulted itself through the wind and waves, oblivious to the fact that Wayne had all he could do to keep himself from being thrown about the cabin while using both hands to complete his tasks. He finally decided to "heave to," which, in simple terms, means to stall the boat by turning it into the wind so that it drifts (relatively) calmly. This made it much easier and safer for him to work.

He finally made the engine happy, but were our problems over? Oh, no, they were not.

Claus radioed us as we neared Bouctouche; they had just docked and were calling to warn us that there were five miles of channel markers to navigate to get to the marina and that we needed to make certain to get there before dark. Wayne looked at the chart and determined that we would arrive around 8:00, just at sunset, so we continued to plug along instead of stopping short of Bouctouche. We reached the outer harbor at 8:00, then realized *we still had five miles, 35-40 minutes, and countless channel markers yet to navigate with daylight vanishing rapidly!* It wasn't obvious from the chart that we were so far away from the marina. At that point, we had no other option but to stay our course—there was no place to anchor—so I grabbed the binoculars to search for the buoys and guided Wayne through them. They would not have been easy to spot under normal conditions, because they were small and easy to confuse with lobster buoys, which dotted the entire channel. Shallow water surrounded us, so if we strayed outside the markers, we would almost certainly run aground.

It was extremely tense and the markers were getting harder to see as light vanished. Claus radioed us with explicit navigational instructions given to him by the harbor master ("Go toward the church steeple, now turn right," and so on). We could hear the controlled panic in his voice. We followed blindly and were guided in by Claus, standing on the break wall with a flashlight. It was the only way we could have found the marina, much less found the entrance and docked. It was pitch black.

By the time we tied up and turned off the engine at 8:45, we could have kissed the dock. Instead, we gave a silent prayer of thanks and gratefully accepted Rachael and Claus's invitation for drinks and snacks aboard *Kyanna*.

Tuesday, September 4, 2007:

A much needed layover

September 4 – It's a good thing today was scheduled as a layover day, because I don't think I could have mustered up the will to sail. We were battered, beaten, and stressed to the max yesterday, both physically and mentally; we were exhausted and just plain bone-weary. Our bodies felt as if we had done a week's worth of sailing in one day. Most people think sailing is a passive activity, but we move around a lot, especially on days like yesterday, and use our core muscles constantly as the body compensates to maintain balance and equilibrium.

Today I used my core muscles to pretty much sit on my butt.

We slept until almost 8:00 and I sat in the cockpit the rest of the morning, editing photos and taking advantage of the strong Wi-Fi signal. I kept falling asleep, though. Sleep deprivation and exhaustion had caught up with me and I didn't accomplish much. Claus and Rachael have electric bikes, so Wayne and Claus stuffed their backpacks full of dirty laundry, got on the bikes, and headed into town to the laundromat. It was our turn to cook dinner, so we made marinated grilled shrimp.

Claus and Rachael informed us today that the inevitable parting-of-ways had come: they had decided to stay in Bouctouche for an extra day or two, but Wayne and I need to leave tomorrow to meet Michael in Charlottetown on Thursday. Claus and Rachael have become such dear friends in the short time we've known them, and we will cherish the experiences, the conversations, the laughter, the hugs, the dinners, the whales, the photos, and countless special moments we've shared on this crazy journey of ours. We will meet up and travel together again, though, possibly even within the next few weeks; meanwhile, we'll have Michael with us for five-and-a-half days to help fill the void.

Wednesday, September 5, 2007:

Sailing at its finest

September 5 – Ahhhh . . . Now, *this* was sailing at its finest. Okay, maybe a bit too much of a good thing with winds at 25-30 knots and 7-8 foot waves, but the winds were in our favor this time and we *flew*. We sailed eighty nautical miles in twelve hours (I know—awfully darn slow to you car-drivers and power boaters) and never turned on our engine until it was time to take down the sails. At that point we experienced several long, heart-stopping minutes when Wayne feared that the propeller had fallen off; he was running the engine in forward but the boat didn't go. The propeller screws on and is held secure with six cotter pins, so it's highly unlikely to fall off. Wayne got it working properly after a few panicky minutes, but we have no explanation for what happened.

We decided to skip a planned stop in Summerside so that we would have a full day tomorrow in Charlottetown. We docked at the Charlottetown Yacht Club.

Sunday, September 9, 2007:

Visit from Michael—he's finally here!

September 6 – Today is the day! I feel like a contestant on the reality show "Survivor" who is getting a visit from a loved one back home!

With Michael arriving tonight and our guest cabin piled with stuff, Wayne and I were highly motivated to get things organized. After one day short of six weeks cruising, believe me, it had to be done. So we stashed away things we aren't using and found better places to put other things.

I wanted to explore Charlottetown, so Wayne sent me on my way while he stayed behind to do laundry and get some boat things done. Charlottetown, Prince Edward Island, is a lovely small city with many historical buildings, and the marina is conveniently located near all the amenities of the downtown area. I walked around town and browsed through the shops for a while, then Wayne and I treated ourselves to badly needed haircuts, went to the grocery store, and had ice cream.

Back at the marina, we finished up the laundry and caught up with email. A shift in the wind made our dockage less than ideal, so the dock master suggested that we move to a better-protected slip. This would give us the added bonus of being farther away from the partiers that kept us awake last night. Although many fishing boats are docked at Charlottetown Yacht Club, none of them appear to be used for fishing anymore; people buy retired fishing boats, fix them up (or not), and use them as recreational or party boats.

Michael's flight got in at 9 p.m. and he took a cab to the marina. We had told him where to find us before knowing we would move, so when he found a 150-foot yacht tied up where *Lena Bea* was supposed to be, he thought we had upgraded!

Michael hadn't eaten dinner, so we went out to a local pub and enjoyed steamed mussels, nachos,

Michael

and beer. Michael also ordered tuna. It is so good to have him with us. Thanks for letting him come, Amy—you get the daughter-in-law of the year award in our book. We wish you could be here, too, of course.

September 7 – We left at 9 a.m. and had to motor because there was no wind. On the plus side, calm water made it easier to spot whales, so Michael was treated to a few sightings on his first day out; he saw quite a few dolphins, as well. We docked for the night in a lovely little place called Ballantyne's Cove, Nova Scotia, just south of Cape George Point.

September 8 – Yesterday and today we've enjoyed warm, sunny weather with calm water and a light breeze. What a change from the 7-8 foot waves and thirty-knot winds we experienced earlier in the week! I guess the variety of conditions prevents boredom.

Later . . . We maneuvered our way through the buoys of St. Andrews Passage, which would have been scenic had it not been foggy. We saw a lone seal swim by the boat. The open water of the Atlantic Ocean welcomed us with more fog and waves. We anchored in a secluded cove dotted with little islands—Yankee Cove, in Whitehead Harbor. While relaxing in the cockpit, we were startled to hear voices; we looked around and saw another sailboat emerge from the fog and come in to anchor nearby. I think they were as surprised to see us as we were to see them. The fog lifted as we ate dinner, revealing the beauty around us.

*In wilderness I sense the miracle of life,
and behind it our scientific
accomplishments fade to trivia.*

~ *Charles Lindbergh*

Sunday, September 9, 2007:

A delightful treat of a day

September 9 – We left around 6 a.m. and sailed until we reached Liscombe Harbor. From there, we motored seven scenic miles through the harbor and up the river to Liscombe Mills. It reminds us of the Boundary Waters Canoe Area in Northern Minnesota. We docked early, at 2:30, which left us plenty of time to explore a bit and take advantage of some of the facilities offered at the resort here, which were included in our dock fee.

We started with a hike and walked past a waterfall, through the woods, and alongside the river; it was a welcome jolt to the senses to be surrounded by trees and the damp, musty smells of moss and pine. I lingered a while to take more photos while Wayne and Michael headed back; Wayne needed to fill the water tank and hose the salt off the boat. We grilled steaks for dinner, then headed up to the indoor heated pool and spa. Mmmmm. It felt heavenly. Today was a splendid treat.

We received an email from Rachael and Claus today: "Hi Michele and Wayne! We hope you're having a great time with Michael. We're still in Charlottetown and we skipped Summerside, too. We miss you! It's very strange not looking out on the water to see where you are and checking in on the radio. We think we'll go to Pictou Harbor tomorrow and see what this tropical storm does. Fair Winds! Rachael."

Monday, September 10, 2007:

Halfway there!

September 10 – We've reached a huge milestone: our approximate halfway point. We've traveled over 2200 nautical miles and have about 2200 more ahead of us.

As we listened to the weather forecast this morning, it became obvious to us that the smart move would be to cancel our plan to go part way and anchor tonight, and instead go all the way to Halifax, about ninety nautical miles. Tropical storm Gabrielle is a couple hundred miles away and not a serious storm, but she's just enough of a nuisance to cause rain and possibly more winds than we care to sail in (30-40 knots). Heavy fog is also predicted for tomorrow, so it does not look like the best day to be on the water. Besides, if we get to Halifax tonight, we'll have a day-and-a-half to sightsee before Michael leaves on Wednesday afternoon.

Having Michael with us has given me the added bonus of a mini vacation from crewing; I am more than happy to let Michael help with the dock lines, fenders, sails and keeping watch. Michael is more of a sailor than I am and enjoys that stuff more than I do, and frankly, I don't mind that Wayne has someone else to boss around for a while. Today it allows me to spend time in the cabin working on photos and updating the blog.

Email from Rachael on September 12: "We're in Port Hawksberry and have rented a car to do the Cabot Trail. We were in Ballantyne Cove last night and heard that you had been there. Be safe with the weather." [Wayne and I were disappointed that we didn't have time to do the Cabot Trail, but in September 2011, in celebration of her upcoming

80th birthday, my mom and I flew to Nova Scotia and did a bus tour, which took us all over Nova Scotia, including Cape Breton Island and the Cabot Trail, as well as Prince Edward Island and a small section of New Brunswick. It was fabulous to see some of what we missed in 2007! Wayne declined our invitation for him to join us.]

Thursday, September 13, 2007:

Tidal Bore, Peggy's Cove, and Halifax

We took a slip in downtown Halifax, Nova Scotia, Monday night and that's where we'll be until tomorrow (Friday). Halifax is an attractive harbor city with culture, history, and character. It offers all the amenities of a big city without being too big, and is easy to get around in on foot.

I'm sitting in the cockpit drinking my coffee, waiting for the boat to heat up so I can take a shower. It was 54 degrees in the boat this morning, too cold for me to shower, but great for sleeping. A couple of mornings it's been down in the 40s, which is perfect with our down comforter.

I find it rather bizarre to sit out here in my bathrobe eating breakfast while watching the people, many dressed in business suits, walk by on their way to work or whatever. They pass by only about thirty feet from the boat, but we're in completely different worlds.

On Tuesday we rented a car for the first time since leaving home. Michael wanted to see the tidal bore in Truro, so we drove up there in the rain.

The Bay of Fundy, which is northwest of Nova Scotia, has the highest tides in the world—some as great as 54 feet! These huge tides cause tidal bores, which form when an incoming tide rushes up a river, developing a steep forward slope due to resistance to the tide's advance by the river, which is flowing in the opposite direction. This causes the phenomenon of the river changing its flow before your very eyes, flowing in over the outgoing river water.

The height of the tidal bore increases with the range of the tide and may vary in height from just a ripple to several feet. It wasn't a dramatic event that day, but impressive nonetheless, considering the unusual phenomenon we witnessed.

Before returning to Halifax, we took a scenic loop around, then continued down to Peggy's Cove, a beautiful postcard town with a lighthouse you have probably seen photos of. Peggy's Cove looks like a movie set, with all the appropriate scenery and props of a fishing village set just so. I'm not convinced anyone really lives there, but there certainly is no shortage of tourists. It was raining, though, so I wasn't able to take many photos.

Tuesday night we went out for lobster dinner; Michael had never eaten whole lobster before, so that was a must-do. He was not disappointed.

Wednesday we walked up to the Citadel and spent a couple of hours there, touring and learning about some of Halifax's military history. After the Citadel, we browsed through some shops so Michael could buy a gift for Amy, then returned to the boat. Michael showered and packed, then it was off to the airport with no time to spare. We enjoyed our time with him tremendously, but it was too short, of course, and there was so much we didn't have time to do. All we can hope is that he had a good time and is glad he came.

After we dropped Michael off, Wayne and I decided to stay an extra day, so we will be here until Friday. Today we are taking a scenic drive down the southwest coast—known as the "lighthouse trail"—to Peggy's Cove (to get the photos I missed on Tuesday), Mahone Bay, and Lunenburg. It appears to be a perfect day for it—sunny skies and temp in the 70s.

Thursday, September 13, 2007:

A souvenir from Nova Scotia

Our scenic drive yesterday was as lovely as we expected. At one point, Wayne pulled the car over so I could take a photo; while returning to the car, I stepped into a deep hole camouflaged with weeds, and fell. I don't know if I hit the camera or a rock, but I was bleeding profusely from a cut just below my lip. We stopped at a restaurant/gift shop so I could clean up, and the proprietor gave me some ice to put on it. I looked  in the mirror and realized I needed stitches, but spent the next few hours in denial with napkins pressed to my lip. Wayne checked the map and saw that there was a hospital in Lunenburg, Fisherman's Memorial Hospital, and suggested we stop there. I wasn't able to talk, smile, eat, or drink without my lip breaking open and bleeding again, so I reluctantly agreed to go. Three stitches, two hours, and one hospital bill later, we were on our way. Admittedly, the stitches really were necessary, so it's a good thing we took care of it.

I did get some good photos today; I'll upload them next time we have internet access, so do check back.

We were glad for the extra day here; a few more days wouldn't have been too many as far as I was concerned, but it is time to move on.

Friday, September 14, 2007:

Blog stuff

Another beautiful day in paradise: clear and calm with temps in the 70s.

We left the dock in Halifax this morning and are en route to what our cruising guide describes as one of the most scenic anchorages in Nova Scotia: Port Mouton.

I'm told there have been a few new people checking the blog lately—if you are one of them, I would like to welcome you and thank you for joining us. I have a few hints to help you enjoy the experience more:

First, if you click on the 2007 section on the righthand column under "archives," you'll be able to scroll through the whole blog without clicking on a different page each time you get to the end of one.

At the bottom of the page is a Google interactive map that shows all the places we have anchored, moored, or docked. You can zoom in really close—sometimes so close you can see details. This is a fun feature since it provides a visual of where we are. I recommend that you click on "view larger map" in blue on the bottom.

Also, I often post messages several days to a week before I get around to posting photos and providing hyperlinks, so it pays to check back to previous posts. Sometimes I even add text to the posts or edit them later if my writing is incoherent (late at night or when I'm rushed, which is usually the case). If you left-click on the photos, you can view them larger in a new window.

Finally, if you'd like to leave us a message, you can do so by clicking the "comment" area at the bottom of any post. If you want to read my response, you may need to check back to the same comment area that you made your comment from. We welcome and respond to all comments (at least I hope I haven't missed any), although sometimes I email a response to people whose email addresses I have.

Saturday, September 15, 2007:

Two anniversaries

September 15 – Today is our wedding anniversary—29 years of marriage. It also marks one year since my grandma, Bernice Shore, died at age 101. It's not a sad thing, the fact that she died on our anniversary; it guarantees that we will never celebrate it again without thinking of her and remembering what a special person she was.

Sunday, September 16, 2007:

Gabrielle and an all-nighter to Yarmouth

Whew! It has been a challenging time here in Shelburne Harbor. We arrived yesterday afternoon under gale force (30-40 knot) winds and driving rain. Tropical storm Gabrielle is making things very unpleasant here! We motored around the harbor for about an hour while considering all our options, unable to get a radio response from the marina. Docking was not an option due to the conditions, and although we attempted to moor, it was far too windy to grab a ball, so we finally anchored. We really wanted to dock so we could connect to shore power and charge our batteries, do laundry, take a real shower and get a few groceries. It is cold and windy, but we will dinghy to the marina and maybe accomplish some of the above; the rest will have to wait until we get to Yarmouth in the morning.

The plan is to leave here tonight at 11:00. Why, you might ask. We need to time our passage to Yarmouth precisely to avoid having strong Bay of Fundy tidal currents working against us. If all goes as planned, tomorrow night will be our last night in Nova Scotia, and yes, Canada.

We've been in Canada since arriving in Port Colburne, Ontario on August 8 (we also had a brief stay in Sault Sainte Marie, Ontario) and will remember it fondly: The cities of Montréal, Québec, Charlottetown, and Halifax . . . the Saguenay fjord . . . the whales, dolphins and seals . . . the small fishing villages of Matane, Sainte Anne-des-Monts, Grande-Rivière, Escuminac, and Ballantyne's Cove . . . many beautiful small towns, harbors, and anchorages . . . and the wonderful people we met along the way, as well as the people we traveled with (Claus and Rachael, Michael). Our only regret is having had to rush through it all.

There are two kinds of people: those who say to God, "Thy will be done," and those to whom God says, "All right, then, have it your way."

~ *C.S. Lewis*

Halifax, Nova Scotia

Chapter 5

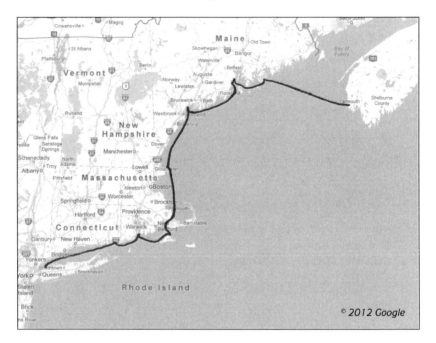

New England

September 17 - September 30

The only way that we can live, is if we grow. The only way that we can grow is if we change. The only way that we can change is if we learn. The only way we can learn is if we are exposed. And the only way that we can become exposed is if we throw ourselves out into the open. Do it. Throw yourself.

~ C. JoyBell C

Monday, September 17, 2007:

Calling Captain Wayne

I have asked Wayne a number of times to post a message to the blog, but he must have decided that he doesn't need to, since I've taken care of it so faithfully and, if I may say so, eloquently. It doesn't occur to him that you might want to hear from him, if only to be reassured that he is still captaining this boat. Because for all you know he could be bound and gagged and sitting in the sail locker . . . or in the belly of one of those big whales . . . or adrift off the shore of Newfoundland in the life raft . . . or he could have jumped overboard weeks ago, unable to endure another moment of my presence.

So I have decided to start a campaign to find out if, indeed, you care to hear from him. If you do, please add a comment at the bottom of this post. Once we have, let's see . . . enough comments, I will pass them on to the captain and see if they are persuasive enough to tear him from his Important Captain Duties and spur him to respond. Come on, people, it's all up to you! I'll throw in a bonus: the person who posts the most persuasive comment, as determined by Wayne, will win . . . something. Ummm . . . I know! A day of cruising with us, but you'll need to get to where we are. And we might not be able to drop you off at a convenient place, although we will try to make sure it's on land. I mean the mainland, but hey! It will be worth it, really! And Wayne will be touched to know how much you care.

From Heidi: "Yes, Wayne—we must hear from you. I was sure you would want to weigh in on several occasions as I've read Michele's eloquent blog, if for no other reason than to rebut some of Michele's side comments (e.g. that Michael's arrival offered the opportunity for her to rest and for you to have someone new to boss around). Surely that merits a rebuttal?"

From Robin: "My dear brother . . . your wonderful wife is so outdoing you in the writing department. Come on . . . we all know you have the ability, let's see it! Just think how much Mom would love it! I am still printing the blog and taking it to her weekly."

Response from Michele: "All right! Keep those comments coming!"

From Tim: "Brow beat Wayne into sharing a few thoughts. He simply has a different perspective to offer. It does not matter how he writes or how he feels about his writing. What he would share will be meaningful and insightful. I would enjoy learning what Wayne looks for when he studies the charts. What does he try to remember? How does that play into the actual sailing? You have referenced some of the challenges but to hear it from the captain would be great."

From Melissa: "C'mon, Captain! Let's hear what you have to say!"

From Bill: "Hey, Wayne, just think how good you would look in a Tartan! Let's hear from YOU! Great sailing to both of you."

Response from Michele: "Bill, Bill, Bill—You say Tartan, I think plaid kilt. NOT a pretty picture AT ALL!" [Bill was referring to a Tartan sailboat, which is what he owns.]

From Donna: "It is time to hear from Captain Wayne! This is your wife's cousin speaking! Blog time, blog time Captain Wayne, show me what you've got! There, I put in my two-cents-worth (please don't pick me, I don't do water too well)."

From Paula: "I was just reading through your blog for the last week and I think back to July 27 and can't believe you're still on the boat all this time except for a few dockings. I surely don't know if I could stand my husband bossing me around that long and I surely would go NUTS with only that little bit of space you've been calling your home! If Wayne doesn't write then we can take only your word that indeed all the things you say about him are true! Hehe! Seriously, I do wonder how most of us could endure—even with all the pleasures—this long of a trip and keep our sanity! Blessings on you both, keep safe, and I hope the rest of the trip is as beautiful as Canada was."

From Tracy: "Wayne, you know, we women have a limited perspective. We write about the way we're feeling, and about people, relationships, all that girly stuff. Now we need the facts. Shelley is talking about 'mooring' and 'dinghies' and stuff like that in the middle of these ponderings, but she forgets the wonderful education you've helped her acquire that we don't have. How about a glossary, and a little sailing tutorial so we know what the heck she's trying to say to us. Interpretation please!

"Then if you want to tell us a little about how you're feeling about your trip so far, the extent to which it's living up to your expectations, your highlights and lowlights, we would love to hear it."

Tuesday, September 18, 2007:

A girl's gotta do what a girl's gotta do

Today is the day my sutures are supposed to be removed, and in the interest of adding a little excitement and suspense to this blog, I have decided to remove them myself. Besides . . . considering I don't see even a speck of land from here, much less a doctor, my options are limited. Have Wayne do it? Surely you're joking. As if I would let him get that close to me with a sharp implement after enduring my companionship 24 hours a day, seven days a week, for seven-and-a-half weeks! I bought some sharp pointy manicure scissors at PharmaSave yesterday, and I have a magnifying mirror and tweezers. Now if I could just get Wayne to make this boat stop rocking long enough to do the deed . . . It would be SO not funny to end up in the ER needing stitches because I accidentally stabbed myself while removing my stitches!

Wayne and I grabbed a few hours of sleep before leaving Shelburne at 11 p.m. Sunday night. I went back to bed once we were out of the harbor and told Wayne to wake me when he needed a break, but he never did. I made the mistake of drinking coffee when we got up to leave at 11:00, so was unable to get to sleep until about 5:00 anyway, but I did sleep until 9 a.m. It has been very cold the past couple of nights, with frost warnings throughout the area. We have instrument displays in two locations, though, so it's as easy to navigate from the cabin as it is from the cockpit, especially at night when radar is necessary to "see" anyway.

An unsung savior on this trip has been our cockpit enclosure; traveling without it would have been downright miserable, even intolerable at times. We are protected from the wind, rain (for the most part), bugs, and sun—a very comfortable way to travel. We can open it up completely, use just the screens or clear panels, or add canvas sections as needed for warmth. As the weather gets colder during the coming weeks, we will be ever more thankful to have it.

We docked in Yarmouth yesterday at around 12:30 p.m. Our arrival coincided precisely with the arrival of the high speed ferry (which travels at forty miles per hour and puts out a huge wake) from Maine, which blasted across our path to make its noon arrival. Wayne had notified Fundy Traffic of our presence, so the ferry captain knew we were there and radioed to let us know when he'd be passing and where we should wait to be out of his way. We'll be crossing paths with the CAT again this morning.

We checked in at the restaurant that manages the dock and Wayne arranged to have fuel delivered to the boat (no fuel pumps here). I did a couple loads of laundry and took a shower, then the two of us went for a walk. There was no Wi-Fi access at the dock, and although we plugged in at the restaurant, we had no luck getting on there, either. Wayne and I grabbed our computers and went up to the library for a while after dinner before going to bed early to prepare for our 2 a.m. departure from Yarmouth.

Our route today takes us from Yarmouth, Nova Scotia, to the Bar Harbor area of Maine. Yes, the next time you hear from us we will be back in the USA!

Wayne is in the cabin getting some much-needed sleep in preparation for our passage tonight.

So here we are. Another gorgeous, cloudless day. We are motoring, but as I've said before, it makes it easy to blog and do other things around the boat. That's as opposed to some of the more intense days of sailing and/or rough water, when it's inadvisable to be down below any more than absolutely necessary or have anything fragile (such as computers) in the cockpit.

Now I will end the suspense and report that yes, I did remove my stitches, and without incident. End of story.

Thursday, September 20, 2007:

An unexpected glimpse of family history

September 18 – Northeast Harbor in Maine is a little town on Mt. Desert Island, also the location of Acadia National Park. We docked shortly before 4 p.m. and settled in. Since it had been a long day (we left Yarmouth at 2:25 a.m.), we were ready for an early night. I went for a walk and stopped at the grocery store before returning to the boat to make dinner.

September 19 – After a good night's sleep, we were ready to explore. L.L. Bean, whose headquarters are in Freeport, Maine, sponsors a free shuttle bus service that will take you around the island. It runs every half hour and you can get on and off as you wish—a wonderful amenity and one we appreciated very much, considering our lack of wheels. We'll show our appreciation to L.L. Bean by stopping in Freeport in a couple of days.

So little time, so much to do. Everyone says you have to go to Bar Harbor, so we did. What we didn't know was that there were two cruise ships docked with a total of 8000 passengers, all converging on this little town of about 5200 people.

We enjoyed our walk around Bar Harbor perusing the shops, but would have appreciated a hike in Acadia more.

Oh well. The drive around the park was beautiful, however, with its ocean and mountain vistas.

We had an unexpected treat in Bar Harbor, though. I saw a little clock shop on Main Street, and since I've always loved clocks, I had to go in. Well, the proprietor, Alexander H. Phillips, was an older gentleman who knows clocks inside and out (literally). He sells and restores antique clocks, so I asked him if he was familiar with McClintock clocks. He enthusiastically started talking about how well-made and desirable they were and pointed out that the bank clock outside was a McClintock, and he was responsible for maintaining it. At one

point the bank was going to tear it down. When one of their wealthy customers heard about it, she said that if they tore down the clock she would withdraw all her money from the bank and so would all her friends.

When I told Mr. Phillips my maiden name was McClintock, that O.B. McClintock was my great-uncle and my grandpa used to work for him, he absolutely insisted—several times—

that I write down as much as I could about the family history, especially as it pertained to the clock company, because nothing is known about it. Unfortunately, I remember nothing and don't know who would. The O. B. McClintock Company of Minneapolis manufactured a complete line of public clocks, many of which were purchased by banks, where they hung from the building or stood outside on main street, USA. Many are still standing in small towns across the country, including Winter Haven, Florida, where my mom lives. The company also manufactured burglar alarm systems. A few years ago I did a bit of research and discovered that in 1948, the company bought the Waltham Electric Clock Co. from the Waltham Watch Company to make electric alarm, kitchen and wall clocks. I bought some of these McClintock clocks on eBay and gave them to my mom and siblings for Christmas that year. They were flabbergasted because no one in the family knew the company made more than just public clocks; I don't even know if my dad knew that. I bought three more on eBay a year or two ago. They were from a jeweler's estate and were new, in the boxes, with the price tags still on them.

This is probably of little interest to anyone but our family, but it adds something new and different to the blog.

September 20 – Today we received a message from Gary DeSantis, the guy we bought our boat from: " . . . It is so incredible that you were able to do this together, and I am so happy for you both. I had a great laugh when Michele wanted  the helicopter rescue from the dreaded spinnaker broach. Been there done that many times racing, but it's not what a cruising sailor enjoys at all.

"So neat how you met up with another couple . . . you have a lifetime of great memories that most people only think about, so I agree that you just have to do it, and with God's help and strength, dreams can come true . . . I need to hang on to this now more than ever. Thanks, Michele, for sharing such a wonderful personal experience so eloquently. God bless and keep you both. Gary."

Tonight we are moored in Camden Harbor, about halfway down the Maine coast, and will explore the towns of Camden and Rockland tomorrow.

Friday, September 21, 2007:

Lobster capital of the world

Today marks eight weeks since Wayne and I left the marina in Bayfield, and we're moored in Rockland, Maine, the Lobster Capital of the World. A celebration is in order, wouldn't you agree? Hmm, what to do, what to do . . . I guess the only question is "Where should we go for our lobster?"

Speaking of lobster, we spent a while visiting with a couple of lobstermen from near Boston; they were fascinated with our journey. Captain Peter Mahoney made us an irresistible offer: if we come and visit him and his wife while in the Boston area, they'd serve us all the lobster we can eat in an evening!

The day started out surprisingly warm and sunny, so we delighted in the beautiful morning as we sat in the cockpit savoring our coffee and breakfast, then took the dinghy into Camden and walked around town. Camden is a quaint seaside town and we found it charming and tranquil. We meandered in and out of the shops, stopped to take photos and enjoy the scenery, and simply reveled in the ambiance.

Wayne and I got back to the boat around noon and ate lunch on our way to Rockland, one of Maine's largest fishing ports. It's a busier harbor, with ferries, fishing boats, and other commercial vessels coming and going, along with private watercraft.

Rockland, Maine

Last night and tonight we've moored rather than docked, which is a lot cheaper—$30 a night instead of $90. So far, the marinas in Maine have been a lot more expensive than the ones in Canada, where the least we paid for a mooring or dock was nothing and the most we paid for a dock was $80 including tax (but only in the big cities; it was typically closer to $40-$50). It will get more expensive as we travel down the East Coast. Some marinas charge as much as $4.50 a foot, so we will anchor and moor when possible, but there's often no option but to dock.

~~~~~~

Friday, September 21, 2007:

And now, FINALLY, a word from the captain

"Wayne here. Well, I really didn't need too much prodding. I wanted to keep a blog with pictures of our journey and Michele agreed to find out how to do it. In the process she took it on as her project, and as you can see, she has done a tremendous job—far better than what you would be reading from me. When we stop in a port or anchor, the first thing we have to do is look for a Wi-Fi connection so she can keep you updated! My only contribution to the blog has been the Google Map that shows where we have been.

"As for Michele's contest, all of you who responded are winners. We really appreciate hearing from you and getting comments. Since you are all winners, just make sure you don't all show up at once!

"Knowing that Michele has kept you current on the details of our trip, I will only add that the experience has far exceeded my expectations. We have enjoyed all the places we have visited, and have especially enjoyed meeting and talking to people we meet.

111

"We have motored more than I would have liked, mostly because there was too little wind or a bad direction and we needed to move on. However, most of the sailing has been wonderful, and often faster than motoring. Sometimes we motor and sail together to gain more efficiency.

"As Michele mentioned in one of her posts, we have become accustomed to the boating routine and what needs to be done. Michele claimed that she is not the sailor and does not know how to operate everything . . . well, *that is history.* She can run the boat quite well now, and we work together very well for docking, anchoring, doing watches, and many other tasks.

"I was concerned about leaving in a new boat with new equipment and electronics that I had installed mostly over the ninety days prior to leaving. We had very little time to learn and test everything before we left. Remember, *Lena Bea* was commissioned May 30 and the first time we had her away from the dock was the weekend of June 30. We took her out again the following weekend, and aside from a couple of short sails with Gary around Bayfield to test the rigging and instruments, that was the extent of it until we left on July 27. We have learned and adjusted along the way, and almost everything has worked well, with only minor problems and adjustments necessary.

"I am delighted with our Island Packet; she sails and motors very well. It is a quality sailboat, beautifully finished, safe, fast, and stable. We appreciate the additional space, comfort, and other features.

"Thank you for reading our blog and sharing our journey. We hope you're enjoying it. If you have other questions, I will be happy to answer them."

Monday, September 24, 2007:

Fun and Games

September 22 – We left our mooring around 6 a.m. in fog that kept getting thicker. As if that wasn't enough fun, we also had to watch for and maneuver around lobster pot buoys and scores of lobster boats. It's not a good feeling to hear a boat engine and be unable to see where it's coming from. We have radar, of course, but that has its own set of challenges and is no substitute for being able to see other boats nearby. Then there's the horn. If you're motoring and visibility is less than half a mile, you are supposed to sound your foghorn  every two minutes. *Lena Bea* has an automatic foghorn that doesn't work because the hailer is out of order, so I had to do it the old-fashioned way: We have an air horn that looks like a water bottle with a contraption on it and you have to pump it up every time you blast it.

So every two minutes for about two hours I watched the clock, blasted the horn, and pumped it back up. While I played "Watch, Blast, and Pump," Wayne played "Dodge the Pot Buoys," "What's That I See on Radar?" and "Is That a Boat Up There?" Yep, it was a morning of fun and games.

It was probably a foolhardy decision to keep going in the fog, but we are in Maine, which is famous for fog, and we could have spent who knows how long waiting for it to lift.

The fog finally lifted, but the fun wasn't over yet. Wayne's favorite game is "Sails Up with Perfect Wind for the Whole Day," but we usually end up playing "Sails Up, Wind Dies, Sails Down." Today it was "Sails Up, Wind Dies, Sails Down, Sails Up, Wind Dies, Sails Down, Sails Up, Wind Dies, Sails Down"—my least favorite game.

Dodging lobster pot buoys

There are three marinas in South Freeport and the first two we called didn't have room for us because they were filled with boats waiting to be hauled out for the season. After a couple of phone calls back and forth, the third one, Ring's Marine Service, told us they had a mooring and explained where to find it. Long story short, first we couldn't find it, and when we finally did, we discovered the rope was too short to reach our boat. Furthermore, a guy on a nearby boat yelled not to tie up there because we would end up dragging. We radioed Ring's and the woman on the other end said she would send her husband down to help us. We played "Idle for an Hour" and "What Do We Do Now?" but no one showed. We finally took out fenders and dock lines and prepared to tie up at the city dock, a game called "Now He'll Come for Sure."

Sure enough, just as I was tying us up at the dock, a guy in a dinghy came by waving and asked if we were waiting for Ring's Marine Service, then motioned us to follow him back to the mooring. He untangled the mooring rope so we could tie up, and assured us it would hold. We asked if the shuttle into Freeport was still running, and he answered, "No, but the Thornton shuttle is." So after we got the boat squared away and dinghied to the dock, Thornton drove us three miles or so into Freeport for a game of "Shop till You Drop or until 10:00, Whichever Comes First," and told us to call him when we were ready to return to the boat. How's that for service?

There are many outlet stores in Freeport, but we buzzed through them quickly and didn't buy anything, unlike the first time we were there back in around 1990. There were very few outlet malls back then, and we went a little crazy. This time we made all of our few purchases at L.L. Bean. We were dismayed to learn that their outlet store had moved a mile away, so we didn't buy very much. The retail store had all fall and winter clothes, which we have plenty of and don't need as much of any more since we spend so much time in Florida. I was hoping to get all kinds of summer stuff on clearance at the outlet, and we could have walked down there, but they closed at 6:00 (unlike the retail store, which is open all the time). We didn't have enough time anyway.

I ended the day with a game of "Searching for Wi-Fi," but I lost and went to bed.

Rockland, Maine

Rockland, Maine

South Freeport, Maine

Camden, Maine

116

Monday, September 24, 2007:

Even a boat needs to be cleaned

September 23 – Wayne is usually up in the morning before me. It doesn't matter what time I go to bed, I don't get up easily before 7:00. Since most days on this voyage have started around 6:00, if not earlier, it has been a struggle for (poor, poor) me, but it takes two of us to get away from the dock and I don't complain.

This morning I heard Wayne get up and asked him if it was foggy. Thankfully, it wasn't. I then dozed as he went about his normal routine of making coffee, checking the weather, and plotting our course for the day. It wasn't necessary this morning, but if it's cold in the cabin (under fifty degrees) Wayne will turn on the heat to make it easier for me to get out of bed. What a guy! This morning I was even less eager than normal to get moving and decided to wait until he came and roused me. When I awoke, it was 8:00 and we were well underway. Since we were moored and it was calm, he didn't need my help and let me sleep. That was a treat.

The extra sleep and the sunny skies energized me enough to clean the inside of the boat. We keep things tidy for the most part, and I clean the galley and heads (kitchen and bathroom to you non-nautical folks) regularly, but I had only dusted once and, aside from an occasional blitz with the hand vac, I hadn't cleaned the floor—yuck! My cleaning frenzy inspired Wayne and he went to work on the cockpit. It feels good to have a clean boat.

Yesterday I wore my winter down jacket much of the day, and today I wore a tank top. What a difference a day can make!

We had some great sailing and anchored in Rockport, Massachusetts, on the tip of Cape Ann at around 5:30 p.m. We took the dinghy in to town and were blown away by the quaintness of this old New England seaport. Really cute little shops and galleries and photo ops left and right. I knew immediately that I wanted to stay tomorrow as well and Wayne agreed with me, but it will require an adjustment to our itinerary.

QUESTION OF THE DAY: "How long have you been sailing? How did you get started? What other boats have you owned?"

Wayne: *I have been sailing since 1978. In 1975, I was in Miami Beach on an IBM awards trip. One of the planned activities was a three-hour sail on a 37-foot Morgan sailboat. I have always been intrigued by sailing, and after this, I was hooked. When I returned to Miami Beach with IBM in 1978, I took a few extra days and chartered the same sailboat with the owner and his wife as captains. Shortly after returning to Minneapolis, I bought my first sailboat, a nineteen-foot Flying Scot, which we sailed on Lake Minnetonka.*

Michele: *We bought it just a couple of months before we got married. A year later we moved to Plymouth and decided to keep the boat on Medicine Lake, which was close to home. We joined the Medicine Lake Sailing Club and learned to race. A couple of years later, we and about twelve other members of the club bought 16-foot MC-Scows to form our own racing class. We raced nearly every Saturday and Sunday (I could only race when I didn't have to photograph weddings) for a couple of years.*

We mostly gave up sailing while we were raising our family, but when they got a bit older, Wayne and a few other guys would occasionally charter a boat on Lake Superior; sometimes they would make it a fathers and sons trip.

In the fall of 1998, Wayne bought Wind Dancer, *a 1995 Island Packet 37. He and the guy he bought it from sailed it back to Bayfield from Toledo, Ohio the following May. We kept her docked at Port Superior Marina in Bayfield, Wisconsin, and sailed her in the Apostle Islands National Lakeshore on Lake Superior. And as you know, we bought* Lena Bea *in November 2006.*

~~~~~

Monday, September 24, 2007:

A semi-spontaneous visit with friends

September 24 – Wayne and I had one of those rare, relaxing mornings when we didn't have to leave at first light or earlier, but I was antsy and ready to explore Rockport. First we needed to refigure our itinerary for the next couple of days, since we had decided to spend an extra night here. We are trying to figure out the best time and place to meet up with my cousin Dave, his wife Mary, and their youngest son Jacob. They are missionaries in West Africa and on home assignment for 7-8 months; they're from

the Twin Cities but are on a driving vacation in parts of the northeastern U.S., visiting friends along the way. When Dave emailed me about meeting up, we jumped at the opportunity. Of course, we aren't able to plan more than a week or so in advance, and even then our plans are subject to change based on winds, weather and whim. First we planned to meet in Maine, then it changed to Cape Cod, with other

possibilities tossed about
in between. On Cape
Cod, we had a series of
three designated meet-
ing locations, based on
where we thought we
could get to at the right

time. Whew! Fortunately, the Deckers are flexible and patient.
I think we've finally nailed it down to Sandwich, Massachusetts,
late tomorrow (Wednesday) afternoon.

Remember John and Diane, the couple we visited in
Vermilion, Ohio? Well, they were attending a wedding in

Cape Cod yesterday
and were headed to
Kennebunkport, Maine,
today. Since they would
be passing by Rockport,
the two guys had discussed
the possibility of meeting
up again. As we walked around town this morning, Wayne
called John. He and Diane were an hour-and-a-half away
and would be stopping in Rockport to see us! Just as easy
as that. See how spontaneous we can be? Not only that,
but they parked the car and there we were, right across the
street! It was so much fun to see them.

The four of us strolled around town, stopped and ate lunch (lobster rolls, yum!), then took a drive to Gloucester and back. It was a beautiful autumn day, spent with great friends in a lovely location. What more could we ask for?

Rockport, Massachusetts

Rockport, Massachusetts

Wednesday, September 26, 2007:

Joyful reunion with the Deckers

September 25 – We had good winds and arrived at the Sandwich Marina on Cape Cod at 2:30, with plenty of time to spare until my cousins came at 4:15. What a thrill it was to see them! Jacob has grown up so much since we saw him last. We also enjoyed meeting their friend and host, Meg.

We visited on *Lena Bea* for a while, then went for a drive to the Sandwich Boardwalk. This boardwalk crosses Mill Creek and beautiful marshes, leading to a lovely public beach on Cape Cod Bay. Stretching over 1000 feet in length, the original wooden walkway was destroyed by Hurricane Bob in 1991. Residents and supporters rebuilt the Boardwalk by selling over 1700 personalized planks. We walked the length of it and enjoyed reading the planks along the way.

Mary and I had a few chuckles over the name of the town, of course, especially when we saw the Sandwich Police. "What do they do?" Mary asked, "Bust people for putting too much mayo on their sandwiches?" Then of course there's the Sandwich Sandwich Shop.

We had dinner at a lovely Victorian Inn called "The Painted Lady" and got partially caught up on each other's lives. We'll see them again before they return to Senegal—on Christmas Eve at our home in Minnesota. This, though, was a special time to visit alone and with no distractions, and we returned to the boat feeling blessed to have had the short time together.

Wednesday, September 26, 2007:

Travel frustrations

Wi-Fi service has been nearly nonexistent the past few days. If I'm lucky, sometimes emails in my outbox will be magically sent when I receive a momentary signal, but that's about it. Right now I am sitting in the marina office because their Wi-Fi signal isn't strong enough to reach the boat. We have often found that to be the case. Due to the size of our boat, the marinas often have us dock near the perimeter, which is usually the farthest point from the office and their router.

The struggle between staying to enjoy our ports of call and needing to move along is a constant, agonizing thing, and for me, the hardest part of this trip (thankfully). A short distance by car can be the equivalent of a day or two by boat, and now that the days are shorter and traffic heavier, we can only do 40-50 nautical miles a day. Once at our destination, we seldom have time to do more than just wander around and take a few photos—forget about seeing any museums or doing any serious hiking. We had to pass up our lobster dinner with lobsterman Peter in Hull, Massachusetts (no time to stop in Boston Harbor), and may have to pass up a visit with Bill and Nancy in Newport, RI, but that remains to be seen. Wayne is still working on our route.

If there's one thing I've learned about myself on this trip, it's that I'm inclined to want to live in the moment—i.e., yes, I know there are other destinations and people awaiting us ahead that are equally important and I don't want to miss them, but we are here NOW and I like THIS place and I want to stay an extra day and are you sure we can't figure out a way to do it all?

That said, I think the hardest part of this trip for Wayne is dealing with me. (Wayne, please feel free to contradict me.)

Sure, I have fantasies about selling the boat and redoing our route by car, but I really should not complain. It has been a fabulous voyage and I need to keep reminding myself that it's also a different kind of trip—not so much about the sightseeing as it is about the experience and the adventure. And we've seen so much by sea that would be impossible to see by land.

Today I was frustrated in a major way. Here we are in Cape Cod with two days and a rental car. We weren't able to get online last night to do any research, and neither of us knows anything about Cape Cod, so we set off this morning with next to no information. I usually like to have information and a plan when I visit a place, and it felt as if I was groping around in the dark. I stopped at a bookshop to find a guide book, but didn't want to pay $15 for way more information than we could possibly use in one day. Wayne was with me at the second bookstore and I relented to buying the guide, partly because the info the shopkeeper gave us was worth the cost of the book; we will also use it Friday when we visit Martha's Vineyard.

It's not fair to base our impression of a place on such a ridiculously short visit. That said, our impression of Cape Cod today was somewhat underwhelming, although we did like Chatham and the drive along 6A, and I can see that the Cape would be a lovely place to rent a cottage on the beach and just chill out for a week or longer. Maybe it was because we have been to so many splendid places the past two months or maybe we just didn't go to the right places today, I don't know. We saw a little of the National Seashore today and will return tomorrow. We've heard good things about it and I don't think we'll be disappointed.

Okay, I think I am all whined out for today. Thanks for your indulgence.

Thursday, September 27, 2007:

New day, new attitude

September 27 – This morning as Wayne scrutinized the chart and our intended itinerary, it became obvious that something had to go. I had already conceded my willingness to trade a stop in Newport, Rhode Island, for an extra night in Mystic, Connecticut, and forgo a layover in New York City entirely, but there were still too many stops scheduled for the time we have.

So we returned the rental car a day early and told the marina we would not be staying an extra night after all, and instead sailed over to Martha's Vineyard. We missed seeing the National Seashore in Cape Cod, but I was okay with that; I told Wayne that I didn't know if it's just the mood I'm in today or whether I'm becoming a bit tired of sightseeing, but right now I just want to move on and get to Florida. Maybe I have simply surrendered the struggle.

Today marks two months since we left the dock in Bayfield.

Wayne is so funny. Every time we go under a bridge, no matter how high it is, he freaks out, afraid that it's not high enough. Our mast is 62 feet and we have yet to go under one that's 65 feet, although dozens await us on the Intracoastal Waterway (I may have to sedate and blindfold the captain). Today's bridge was 120 feet and he told me to be sure to pass under the middle of it because it's a little higher there. I tease him and tell him that he thinks his mast is way taller than it really is.

Our passage through Cape Cod Canal was less than ideal because we had strong southwest winds opposing the tidal current. The combination created sharp, steep waves, making for an uncomfortable ride. On the southwest end of Cape Cod is Woods Hole, and the channel there is narrow with many turns, confusing channel markers, and notoriously strong currents. Wayne had to fight 4-5 knots of current from the side along with 15-25-knot winds from the same direction, which slowed us down and wanted to push us sideways. That, along with rocks off our starboard side and shallow water off the port side, and there was no room for error. We snaked our way through without incident, due to Wayne's impeccable piloting skills and my acute vision for spotting markers.

While we were at the fuel dock at Tisbury Wharf in Vineyard Haven, I got online (strong signal—yeah!) and reserved a rental car so we could do a quick tour of Martha's Vineyard. We left at about 4:30 and went directly to Memensha, a simple, serious fishing village. In fact, it's one of several island locations featured in the movie "Jaws." During our journey I've developed a deep fondness and fascination with rustic, smelly, fishing villages, and this one fit the bill. It reminded me of Peggy's Cove near Halifax, but it's more authentic and not touristy.

I don't know what it is about old lobster traps, dilapidated fishing shacks, and grungy fishing trawlers that bring out the photographer in me, but they do and Memensha had it all, with a bonus. There was a woman there, a full-time artist who also teaches architectural drawing (by hand!) in the architecture school at Harvard. She gave me permission to photograph her and I thought she was a fascinating subject. I loved how the red and blue in her clothing mirrored the red and blue of the barrels and fishing shack in the background.

Edgartown looked like a lovely little town, as refined as Memensha is crusty, but not in a pretentious way. We didn't even get out of the car, though, because it was starting to get dark and we were hungry.

Wayne and I had a hankering for some Mexican food, so we headed for the only Mexican restaurant we knew of on the island, Sharky's Cantina in Oak Bluffs. As we waited to be seated, another couple came over to wait near us. The woman and I immediately recognized each other—Noreen works in the office at the marina! One of two people I've met on the island, hundreds of restaurants . . . what are the chances? We struck up a conversation with her and her friend Steve, the captain of a small luxury cruise ship currently docked in Vineyard Haven. Our table was ready and there was room for four, so we invited them to join us. Captain Steve shared stories of how he unintentionally became a commercial fisherman after a night of drinking too much, and how he made the transition to cruise boat captain. He also had some great tips for navigating the East Coast and places we should stop; Wayne took notes.

Captain Steve advised us against lolly-gagging around, and strongly recommended that we look for a favorable weather window and do a straight shot from NYC to the Delaware and Chesapeake Bays. This time of year the weather can get quite nasty off the New Jersey coast, and we want to be in the protection of the Intracoastal Waterway if that happens.

Four hours later we dropped off the rental car, pleased as we could be with our short time in Martha's Vineyard, and glad we chose it over another day in Cape Cod.

Friday, September 28, 2007:

Searching for mooring #355

We decided to stop in Newport after all, and thought we were in good shape as we entered the harbor at around 1:45, because it was early enough that we would have the better part of the day in town for a change. First we needed to find mooring #355, which Bill and Nancy (whom we met in Québec City) graciously offered to let us use. Now, by some accounts, Newport, Rhode Island, is the sailing capital of the U.S. The harbor is huge and moorings are everywhere. Trying to find a specific mooring is like trying to find a contact lens in the grass on a dewy morning. Wayne left a message for Bill after trying unsuccessfully to reach him on either his home or cell phone. Meanwhile, he motored around while I peered through the binoculars trying to find Bill's mooring. We did this for about half an hour before Bill called back and told us more specifically where it was. Great, now we'll find it . . . NOT. Motored around for another half hour and finally located Bill's mooring . . . ATTACHED TO ANOTHER BOAT!

Our cruising guide lists a dizzying array of wharves, docks, and piers in Newport Harbor, so we randomly called one to arrange for a mooring (for $45—dang!). By the time we finally got hooked up, it was 3:00; that's fine, we will still have plenty of time in town. Except Wayne decided that he needed to CHANGE THE OIL, but it would only take about half an hour . . . RIGHT. That's fine, I'll just get online and update the blog while I'm waiting . . . SURE THING.

Now, I don't dare ask the captain why it took THREE HOURS to change the oil, nor do I even want to know. But the job is done, I never did get online, and we're FINALLY in the dinghy on our way to the wharf at 6:00, but when we get to the wharf we realize WE DON'T HAVE A FLASHLIGHT (a critical tool for finding your boat after dark in a mooring field of a gazillion other boats) so Wayne has to go back to the boat and get one . . . and IT'S 6:15!

Wayne's rebuttal: "Three-hour oil change . . . not exactly! It did take about an hour to change the oil and filter, but I had to spend an additional hour cleaning up oil that leaked while removing the filter. This is under the engine in a very difficult area to reach, and I have to hang over the generator upside down to get at it. It was, however, three hours from the time we picked up the mooring until we left the boat."

Add Newport to the list of destinations we'll return to by car someday.

Saturday, September 29, 2007:

Prestigious company in Newport Harbor

We had some very prestigious company in Newport Harbor last night, and some diligent Homeland Security folks who were intent on protecting her: the *Queen Mary 2*. We

were just minding our own business as we made our way out of the harbor and this Coast Guard boat with a machine gun came along next to us as if

to keep us from getting any closer. I hope this was just routine Homeland Security or some VIP on board rather than an imminent threat.

The Newport waterfront was one hopping place last night! I can only imagine what it must be like at the height of the season. Since leaving Nova Scotia and Maine, it feels as if we've jumped backward in time from October to August; the tourists seem to be enjoying one last hurrah and the boaters around here do not appear ready to call it quits.

Of course, great weather makes all the difference in the world. Although we've been about a week ahead of good fall color, we have been blessed with gorgeous weather and today was no exception. Perfect winds and favorable currents moving us along at 9-10 knots made today one of the best on the water for us. Our hull speed (maximum speed under sail for our boat) is 8.5 knots. I sure hope this is the day Claus and Rachael are crossing from Nova Scotia to Massachusetts.

We've docked our rig in Mystic, Connecticut, for the night. I wish we could spend more time here, but we will move on tomorrow to Huntington Bay, Long Island (Good thing you didn't wait around for us, huh, Greg and Darlene?) before passing through New York Harbor on Monday, which we anticipate to be another highlight of the trip.

Suzanne decided to attend that conference in Philadelphia from October 8-10 and will join us for the weekend on October 5. Suzanne has never sailed with us before, never even seen *Wind Dancer* or *Lena Bea*, and of course Wayne and I are thrilled that she wants to hook up with us! After she leaves us on Sunday we plan to stop in Annapolis, Maryland, (in the Chesapeake Bay) for the last day of the Boat Show on Monday.

Sunday, September 30, 2007:

The captain answers some questions

Thank you for the encouragement you gave Wayne and all the great questions you asked him though the comments section and emails. Here are some of his responses:

QUESTION: "I would enjoy learning what Wayne looks for when he studies the charts. How does that play into the actual sailing? You have referenced some of the challenges but to hear it from the captain would be great."

Wayne: *I look for hazards to navigation such as shallow water, rocks, and strong currents. I use the charts to plan our route and use the aids to navigation such as buoys, markers, lights, tall structures on land, and islands. I take mental note of hazards and usually stay well clear unless we must pass closer to go through a channel. This allows us to relax more.*

When approaching a harbor or channel, I study the charts ahead of time to know what to expect. I enter information into the chart plotter so compass headings are readily available to provide headings. I always identify buoys as far ahead as possible. Often both of us will look for the channel buoys and markers in difficult areas. Binoculars are an essential tool to help locate buoys ahead.

Another challenge is entering a strange marina and trying to locate a slip, then being prepared to dock in a tight area with currents and wind.

Michele: *Wayne is extremely cautious and an expert sailor, navigator, and pilot. It sure makes life on the water less stressful for me!*

QUESTION: "Just wondering how the mechanics (engine, generator, A/C) have been operating for you. Other than the seaweed, any other problems? Have you been satisfied with the generator? With all the tasks on the boat, what have you had to keep your eye on? Have you used all your sails at the same time?"

Wayne: *The mechanics have been great (except for that seaweed issue). I already have 430 hours on the engine! It has performed extremely well and provided plenty of additional power on a few occasions when needed to fight five-knot currents and strong winds.*

I did have a few problems with the air conditioner water pump not working until I lowered the raw water strainer to keep it below the intake water level.

The generator has been great. We only have about thirty hours on it, but it has worked perfectly since I replaced the damaged heat exchanger before leaving Bayfield.

The other problem we had was an intermittent battery charger that completely stopped working about two weeks ago. Island Packet promptly sent a new charger, covered by warranty, to the Summit North Marina where we will be the next couple of days (What great service!).

I keep a close eye on the Racor filters (a pre-engine fuel filter and water separator), and had to drain water from them three times during the first couple of weeks, but there have been no problems since then. I believe it was due to condensation in the near-empty fuel tank over a couple of winters.

Besides doing scheduled maintenance, I routinely check for leaks, water and oil levels, loose nuts and pins, etc. All the electronics have worked great except the hailer on the ICOM 504 VHF (Michele wrote about this on one of her posts from Maine), which I have not had time to figure out.

I have had the main, genoa, and stay sails all up on a couple of occasions.

**The world will never starve
for want of wonders,
but only for want of wonder.**

~ G.K. Chesterton

Gloucester, Massachusetts

Rockport, Massachusetts

Chapter 6

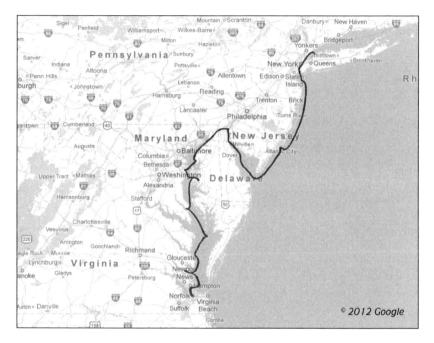

© 2012 Google

New York City through the Chesapeake

October 1 - October 17

Grace has to be the loveliest word in the English language. It embodies almost every attractive quality we hope to find in others. Grace is a gift of the humble to the humiliated. Grace acknowledges the ugliness of sin by choosing to see beyond it. Grace accepts a person as someone worthy of kindness despite whatever grime or hard-shell casing keeps him or her separated from the rest of the world. Grace is a gift of tender mercy when it makes the least sense.

~ Charles R. Swindoll

Wednesday, October 3, 2007:

Amazing Grace

September 30 – One definition of the word "grace" is "the free and unmerited favor of God," and we have experienced God's grace every day of this journey. We've seen it in countless ways, large and small. Here are some examples from today:

Back in August, Greg and Darlene scheduled a trip to New York, planning to meet up with us and visit friends in Rochester and some of Darlene's friends and relatives on Long Island (where she grew up). Unfortunately, we missed them because they left here two weeks ago while we were still in Nova Scotia. Wayne called his brother Greg yesterday afternoon and told him we were finally in Long Island and where we planned to put up for the night. Greg told him that Darlene's friend Laura runs Brewer Marina in Glen Cove, ten miles past our planned destination, and that she would be able to put us up there. Cool! A little while later Wayne got a phone call from Laura, and we were all set. She even gave us a discount! This was God's grace at work.

Mike met us when we docked at Brewer Marina at 6 p.m., which was closing time. He got us squared away and I put in a couple of loads of laundry. I had intended to do laundry in Mystic, but forgot, and was concerned about how soon we would have another chance. This too was God's grace at work.

While I was taking care of the laundry, Wayne chatted with a guy on the dock who shared some local knowledge with him regarding our route—where to go and not go—God's grace at work.

This morning we went up to the office to meet Laura and she offered us the use of her car. We had tried to buy groceries in Mystic, but there was only a small store which didn't have much of what we needed. As with doing laundry, I wasn't sure when we'd have another chance to buy groceries, and again—God's grace at work.

I marvel at how God has blessed us with weather far better than we could have hoped for, and not a day passes that we are not aware of him protecting us. It is quite remarkable how I often feel as if we're in a protective bubble where nothing can touch us. We know that many of you are praying for us—that God would keep us safe and give us favorable weather—and that means the world to us. YOU are God's grace in action, another undeserved blessing for which we praise him and give him (and you) thanks.

Wayne and I have experienced God in many ways over the course of our lives, and now as our Cruise Director. Thank you God, for your "free and unmerited favor" . . . on this trip and always.

Wednesday, October 3, 2007:

New York, New York!

October 2 – Watching the New York skyline gradually emerge from the horizon as we traveled down the East River yesterday was a surreal experience that gave me goose bumps. What a vantage point we had, cruising along the east side of Manhattan, under the Brooklyn and other bridges, and past the Statue of Liberty! It definitely qualified as a trip highlight. We welcomed the change of scenery, as lovely as it's been, for the variety it provided. We decided against a stopover there because we have been to New York City, and one or two nights would only be a tease.

You will no doubt be relieved to know that Homeland Security is alive and well, protecting you from the likes of us (their cohorts in Newport must have warned them). The Coast Guard escorted us in a low-key manner (no one staffing the machine gun this time) along portions  of the East River, especially near the major bridges.

Tonight we will anchor just south of New York City at Sandy Hook and tomorrow night we will be in Atlantic City. We weren't planning to stop there, but apparently there are only a couple of places to stop along the Jersey coast and Atlantic City is our best choice tomorrow.

Rachael called this morning to let us know they finally arrived back in the U.S. last night, having crossed all the way from Lockeport, Nova Scotia, to Marblehead, Massachusetts. They had great conditions and made the crossing in good time—what, 38 hours? 30-some hours, anyway. It is becoming less likely that we will meet up with them again on this trip, since we have a deadline and they do not, but we will probably see them in the Bahamas or somewhere in the Caribbean.

We were upset yesterday by news of a senseless tragedy—a friend of Wayne's and brother in Christ, Chris, was robbed and beaten and died at the hospital. We don't know the details. Wayne feels sick that he can't be there, but our heartfelt sympathy and prayers go out to his family and friends. We also pray that justice will be served.

Thursday, October 4, 2007:

More replies from the captain

QUESTION: "Yes, Wayne—we must hear from you. I was sure you would want to weigh in on several occasions as I've read Michele's eloquent blog, if for no other reason than to rebut some of Michele's side comments (e.g. that Michael's arrival offered the opportunity for her to rest and for you to have someone new to boss around). Surely that merits a rebuttal?"

Wayne: *Just call me Captain Bligh! I know Michele is just being facetious, but since there are only two of us, we must work together for many things that require (or at least are a lot easier with) two people, such as docking. When Michael was here, Michele could relax more or sleep in while Michael helped, or we could divide the duties among the three of us.*

Michele: *Besides, I didn't want to deprive Michael of all the fun! He's like his dad and loves to sail.*

Michael and I have both learned that Wayne is not really "bossing us around." It's just that he's in charge, knows what needs to be done, and has to communicate that to us so we can help. I must say, though, that I am learning the ropes (no pun intended) on this trip. He doesn't need to "boss me around" nearly as much as he did at the beginning.

QUESTION: "I think we need to hear from Wayne as to the relational qualities this brings out in one's life—mainly dealing with only his wife and the boat for so long. How does this help or hinder one's Christian values—like being servants to one another as Christ served back in His day?"

Wayne: *We have learned to work well together in handling the boat and doing necessary chores. We also take turns on watch, so each of us has free time to read, nap, work on the blog, email, plan our route, and study our next locations. Our Christian values certainly help in our relationship. We do respect and appreciate what the other contributes, and often help and serve each other.*

Michele: *After 29 years of marriage, there are very few surprises. We wouldn't have chanced this trip if we weren't sure we could get along. Having said that, we are a normal couple and have our "less than pleasant" moments, but they are thankfully few, and usually happen when we're tired or frustrated. When you know you're going to be together 24/7 for three or four months and are taking the trip of a lifetime, you want it to be a pleasant experience and have great memories of it when it's over. That does not happen by accident. We have both put a great deal of effort into making it a pleasant and enjoyable trip for the other. For instance, although I love being a passenger on the boat, Wayne enjoys all the mechanics of sailing more than I do. He is very sensitive to that, which I appreciate, and doesn't demand much "heavy lifting" from me in that regard, although I help out as needed.*

It's really no different from marriage in general, in that it requires give and take on both sides to make it work.

Never go on trips with anyone you do not love.

~ *Ernest Hemingway*

144

Thursday, October 4, 2007:

A long, hot day in the Delaware Bay

We left at 4:25 a.m. and spent Tuesday night in Atlantic City, docked at the Senator Frank S. Farley State Marina, aka Trump Marina-Hotel-Casino. Of course, we had to take a walk on the boardwalk, so we rode the Jitney bus as far as Trump's Taj Mahal. The Board-walk was

. . . interesting, but not one of those places Wayne had to drag me away from.

After we returned to the marina, Wayne went back to the boat and I went in the casino and played the penny slot machines for an hour or so.

We left Atlantic City Wednesday morning at 6:45 in heavy fog. We discussed whether we should stop in Cape May, NJ, which would leave us with over seventy nautical miles to travel on Thursday, or go all the way to Summit North Marina on the C & D Canal (which connects the Delaware and Chesapeake Bays). Wayne called the marina to find out if there was an intermediate place to stop in the Delaware Bay; they confirmed what we'd been told: that there was not.

They assured Wayne that docking after dark would not be a problem though . . . that the canal and the marina were well lit and easy to navigate, with good depth and no hazards. Wayne also checked tides and currents and determined that they were in our favor for travel that day, so we went the distance. We made the hundred-mile trip in about fourteen hours and docked uneventfully, although Summit North Marina was not as well lit as we were led to believe, and a spotlight was necessary to find our way to the dock.

Now we have a day and a half to catch our breath and get some things done before Suzanne joins us Friday afternoon. We are so excited to see her!

It's been very warm the past couple of days! We had the boat totally opened up for the first time since mid-August, and slept comfortably the past two nights with just a sheet over us. Low temperatures of 65 degrees in October? Toto, I don't think we're in Minnesota anymore! Chances are that from this point on, very cold weather should not be an issue. We are also in the Intracoastal Waterway now, which affords us greater protection from bad weather.

Thursday, October 4, 2007:

Busy, busy blogger

I've been a busy blogger today, as you may have noticed. I added several posts (including more questions and answers from Wayne), amended a couple of previous posts, and uploaded photos. I added a definition of "nautical mile" to the right under our email address, and added a link to a sailing glossary under "links" (which I will be referring to myself).

QUESTION OF THE DAY: "How do you determine
when to anchor and when to moor?"

Wayne: *We anchor whenever we can. Sometimes all the space
in a harbor is full of moorings and there is no room to anchor,
or the wrong conditions exist, such as poor holding or water
that is too shallow or deep.*

Saturday, October 6, 2007:

"Pristine Gall Bladder?"

My stomach and throat had been bothering me for a
few days, but I didn't think much of it until Friday morning
when I awoke with a very sore and swollen throat. The pain
in my stomach grew worse as the day wore on, and by the
time Suzanne called to say she was about 45 minutes away, I
could barely drag myself to the shower. We visited for a while
when she arrived, then I started vomiting (no correlation). I
could not prepare the dinner I had planned and sent Wayne
and Suzanne up to the marina restaurant without me. I laid
down for an hour, unable to sleep or move as the pain increased
to an "8" on the scale of 1-10. I finally called our clinic at
home to see what they thought I should do, and of course the
nurse told me to get to the emergency room.

Well, I certainly did not think an ambulance was necessary,
so the security guard came and got me on the golf cart—
there's no way I could have walked—and drove me to the restaurant, where Wayne and Suzanne were just starting dinner.
Wayne called a cab, for which we waited about half an hour,
then drove for half an hour to Christiana Hospital in Newark,
Delaware; by this time I was in agony and seriously second-
guessing the ambulance thing.

My heart sank as we walked into the jam-packed ER, but mine was the first name called, and they got an IV and pain medication in me as quickly as they could. In the end, all the lab work came back normal, and as she did the ultrasound on my abdomen, the doctor declared my gall bladder to be "pristine." They think it was a case of gastritis—an irritation in the stomach lining without an ulcer [After a couple of recurrences, I was later diagnosed with an ulcer]—and believe the sore throat was caused by stomach acid backing up. That makes sense, because it was unlike any other sore throat I have had.

We returned to the boat at 2:30 a.m., sorry that we had to abandon Suzanne our first of two evenings with her, but thankful that I did not need to be admitted for something more serious.

Two trips to the ER in less than a month! And to think I've only had one other in my adult life, 22 years ago. I should be covered for a long time now, right?

We left the dock at 9:45 this morning and went to North Point Marina in Rock Hall, Maryland.

Suzanne

Sunday, October 7, 2007:

Annapolis Boat Show

We just docked in Annapolis and are right in the heart of the boat show—Yacht Basin Company, slip 75. If you happen to be at the boat show and are checking this blog, please come look us up.

Tuesday, October 9, 2007:

Two visits and repairs in Annapolis

We're still in Annapolis (where it is ghastly hot), having spent two partial days at the Annapolis boat show, the largest sailboat show in the world. Suzanne enjoyed looking at all the different boats with us on Sunday before leaving at 6 p.m. to go to her conference.

We started the day Monday by meeting up with another Island Packet couple for breakfast at Chick and Ruth's. Wayne knows Hayden and Radeen through the Island Packet email list that he has participated on for years, so it was especially fun for him to finally meet them. They had great suggestions on where to go in the Chesapeake, which we intend to follow up on.

We perused the boat show for a few hours and found some things for the boat that we didn't know we needed (naturally).

Around 3:00 we had visitors—Dan and Barbara. Dan, who retired in August, was a business associate of Wayne's for over 25 years. An interesting bit of trivia that Dan, Barbara, and Wayne have in common: all three of them are half Sicilian. We enjoyed a fabulous dinner at one of their favorite restaurants.

Right now Wayne is finishing up repairs on a couple of things that have plagued us from day one: He found out the power supply for the VHF radio hailer was bad, so he had to replace the entire VHF radio. He determined that the battery charger had a faulty circuit breaker. It worked intermittently, which made the problem hard to diagnose, but it has worked perfectly since he replaced it.

Now we are preparing to head over to St. Michael's and will anchor there for the night.

Tuesday, October 9, 2007:

Gotta 'fess up

It never occurred to me for a second that this would happen, but there's something on the blog that at least three people have misunderstood and has me all but rolling on the floor laughing. The section on the right, "Read what the critics are saying about the *Lena Bea* blog?" Well, "the critics" are . . . is . . . me! That's why they are all signed "anonymous." I guess I have to take it as a compliment, though, because I wouldn't have fooled anyone if it were too far from the truth . . . RIGHT? But really—"The most compelling boating adventure since 'Gilligan's Island?'" Have these people ever *seen* "Gilligan's Island?"

You've probably figured out my sense of humor by now and are no longer fooled, if you ever were. Thanks for the belly laughs (you know who you are); I guess the joke was on me.

Read what the critics are saying about the *Lena Bea* blog:

"The blogosphere equivalent of a page-turner! It will leave you clutching your mouse in suspense!"
~ Anonymous

"Gather the family around the computer with a bowl of popcorn! This heartwarming romp aboard the Lena Bea is fun for all ages!" ~ Anonymous

"Destined to be a classic, right alongside *Moby Dick* and *Mutiny On the Bounty!*" ~ Anonymous

"An emotional ride on the open seas that will keep you coming back for more!" ~ Anonymous

"*Lena Bea* is the most compelling boating adventure since 'Gilligan's Island!'" ~ Anonymous

"A spirited saga of two savvy sailors, steaming with suspense and surprises!" ~ Anonymous

"This could be the blog of the year, if not the decade!" ~ Anonymous

"Two sails up!" ~ Anonymous

Wednesday, October 10, 2007:

Seasickness

QUESTION OF THE DAY: "Do you ever get seasick?"

Wayne: *Interestingly, I am prone to motion sickness, but have never been seasick. I have learned how to avoid and/or reduce the effect of motion. After a few days on the boat, we get used to the motion, but I know that I could still get seasick if conditions were bad enough. Michele can actually go down in the cabin and read in rough seas!*

Michele: *I got seasick once, when we went deep sea fishing with Wayne's grandfather and his brother, Greg. I never want to experience that again!*

That said, I also know I could get seasick again under the right (or wrong) conditions. But just as I learned many years ago—the hard way—not to look out the side windows while riding in a car on a curvy mountain road, there are things we do to avoid seasickness. For instance, look at the horizon, do not watch the waves, and spend minimal time in the cabin when it's rough. I can be in the cabin if I lie down and close my eyes, though. And Wayne is right—I can go down in the cabin and read if it isn't too rough. If I must be down below for very long under rough conditions, I'll sometimes pop a piece of ginger gum as a preventive measure; I have also used Motion-Eaze, an herbal formula that you dab behind your ears, which works really well. We have other remedies and preventives, including Sea Bands (acupressure bands for the wrists), but have not felt the need to use any of them yet. We don't use Dramamine or the like.

Many people believe seasickness is mostly psychological.

Wednesday, October 10, 2007:

Trip burnout? Bulb burnout?

This afternoon as we approached Solomon's Island, a highly recommended destination in the Chesapeake Bay, Wayne asked me what I wanted to do there after we anchored. Honestly? Nothing. I just wanted to stay on the boat. So we dinghy to shore, walk around town, and return to the boat hungry and too tired to make dinner. No thanks—that routine is getting old. We have been to so many great places, and I am sure this is a great place to visit as well, but . . .

I'm tired. I am even tired of taking photos, as you may have noticed by the lack of new ones on the blog recently. If I could snap my fingers and be in Punta Gorda tomorrow, I would not hesitate. Don't get me wrong—I'm certainly not desperate to be done with the trip—I'm still enjoying it, but the novelty has worn off, the finish line is in sight, and I will be ready when the time comes.

So what did we do for fun? I got to go up to the top of the mast!

Wayne thought our anchor light was burned out, and going up is probably his least favorite thing to do. I, on the other hand, have been waiting for the opportunity, so I grabbed the new bulb and our little camera and Wayne helped me into the bosun's chair (harness). He then hoisted me very carefully, using the electric winch.

It wasn't quite as much fun being at the top of the mast when a power boat zoomed by, leaving a wake that rocked the boat wildly.

I got to the top and realized I couldn't reach high enough to change the bulb, but before Wayne lowered me down I spent a few minutes basking in the view from 62 feet up and took some photos. I then hoisted Wayne and he changed the bulb, which was not even burned out after all (it turned out to be faulty, which explained why it worked intermittently).

Thursday, October 11, 2007:

Just when we thought we had seen it all . . .

Thursday, October 11 – A rain shower and wind heralded in a cold front during the night, bringing relief from a week of oppressively hot, humid weather. We turned off the fan and dug out the down comforter again.

Wayne had the sails up before we left the harbor, not wanting to waste a minute of the strong winds beckoning to carry us to Tangier Island, Virginia. With winds at 18-24 knots and gusting higher, we averaged eight knots.

Of course, the downside of such winds is docking this monster (Have I mentioned the boat weighs about twenty tons with full tanks of fuel and water?) There were three guys on the dock at the Parks Marina to help us, though, thank goodness!

I had very little experience helping to dock a boat before this trip, and believe me, it's been the cause of many of our most stressful moments! Each docking is different because no two docks are the same, the conditions vary greatly, and whoever is helping you (if there's anyone at all) may or may not know what they're doing. I have never been at the helm when we docked and I don't care to be, either.

This little town is in a class by itself, as described in this quote from the Wall Street Journal Online, dated September 22, 2007:

"Life on Chesapeake Bay's Tangier Island hasn't changed much over the centuries. There's no bridge to the mainland. Locals speak with a distinct dialect, which can be traced back to the island's earliest settlers from 17th-century Cornwall in England. Life revolves around fishing, church and chatting with neighbors over white picket fences . . .."

"It's the local culture that makes this place so fascinating. Most people here can trace their ancestry back to the 17th century, when John Crockett is said to have settled the island with his children. Today, most are at least distantly  related and have one of a few last names—Crockett, Pruitt and Parks are the most common. Many families live in homes passed down for generations, complete with ancestors buried in the back yards . . . "

 Yes, you read that right: Many homes have their own graveyards, and some would be perfect as a set for a horror movie. This would be one creepy town on Halloween.

". . . Now, this quaint way of life is under threat. Crabbing isn't paying the bills anymore, and many watermen are leaving to find jobs elsewhere. Some parents worry that, for the first time, their kids won't have any reason to stay when they grow up."

Okay, so the kids decide to leave the island and put the house on the market. This inquiring mind has questions: What happens with the ancestors? How do you market a home with its own graveyard? Who would buy a house with someone else's dead relatives buried in the front yard (and

you thought that mauve carpet was a deal-breaker)? Finally, how would said ancestors feel if they knew they had been abandoned to continue decomposing in some stranger's front yard? That would be grounds for some serious haunting, if you ask me.

It boggles the mind.

We had to wait for the winds to die down before leaving the marina on Tangier Island, but they were still 18-25 knots with 3-5 foot waves.

Friday, October 12, 2007:

Tow, tow, tow your boat . . .

Lena Bea's First Grounding—Friday, October 12, 2007 in Deltaville, Virginia, just outside of Dozier's Regatta Point Yachting Center. I'd better let the captain tell you about this.

Wayne: "Well, as the saying goes, it is not if, but rather when, you will go aground. After all the difficult areas we have been in, I certainly didn't expect to go aground in the middle of a well-marked channel, going to a marina with many other sailboats (usually a good sign of adequate depth). As usual, I had even checked with the marina before entering, but they didn't warn us and we got stuck in four feet of water in a boat with a five-foot draft.

"Fortunately, the bottom is mud, so there was no damage to the boat. *Lena Bea* has a modified full keel with great protection for the rudder and propeller. We also have unlimited towing service with BoatUS. Several years of membership fees quickly paid for themselves as BoatUS arrived in less than thirty minutes and pulled us out. After getting us free, he towed us through another shallow area and pulled us out again through that. He told us this channel  was a major problem. I'm disappointed that the marina was not better informed (it is a very large major marina in the area), and I spoke with them about the problem when we finally got in.

"Now I have to figure out how we're going to leave without getting stuck again. We will leave at high tide to get an extra eight inches of depth (we were at about mid-tide coming in), and talk to more locals, who usually know the best route through the channel."

Saturday, October 13, 2007:

Deltaville to Gloucester Point, Virginia

After we docked, licked our wounds, and checked in yesterday, we decided to have dinner out. We asked the woman in the office where to go and she suggested a place. The restaurant offers shuttle service between there and the marina, so she gave them a call and arranged for us to be picked up at 6:45.

We were waiting in the drive when our shuttle pulled in, driven by an elderly couple with a Yorkshire terrier. Come to find out, Virgil and Myrtle are the parents of the restaurant owner and it's their 61st wedding anniversary. The dog is not theirs—they were dog sitting for restaurant patrons who did not want to leave him in the car while they dined. Now, that—dog sitting and running a shuttle service for their son's customers on their wedding anniversary—is parenting above and beyond the call of duty.

The service went downhill from there and the food was so-so. All was not lost, however, because we met another sailing couple, Sarah and Roger (a self-proclaimed match.com success story), and had a pleasant visit with them before and after dinner. They ended up following us back to the marina for a look-see at the boat.

In an attempt to avoid a recurrence of yesterday's mishap, we decided to leave at high tide today, about 11:30. I knew immediately what to do with our free morning, as I had noticed a flyer advertising the Holly Point Art and Seafood Festival. We borrowed the marina's courtesy car and had a lovely hour browsing the art booths, watching the Renaissance-costumed performers, and just enjoying the folksy atmosphere.

We had to partake of the seafood portion, of course; I savored the best shrimp salad ever, while Wayne opted for the barbecue.

Now we're docked at York River Yacht Haven in Gloucester Point, Virginia, where we will be until Tuesday or Wednesday. Tomorrow my cousins, Karen and Diane and Diane's husband, Terry (who live in Williamsburg), will pick us up and we'll spend the day with them. We are really looking forward to that!

Wednesday, October 17, 2007:

Connecting with cousins

Wednesday, October 17 – Today we leave Gloucester Point, Virginia, where we've stayed since Saturday evening. It was such a delight to reconnect with my cousins. Diane and Terry moved their family to the East Coast about twenty years ago and Karen moved out here with her son Charlie about ten years ago (I hope I have those years right). We've seen them on occasion when they've returned to Minnesota to visit, but only at funerals and other large family gatherings. Before they moved, we didn't see them much more than once a year at the annual Christmas party, so it was special to have time with just them.

Karen, Diane, and Terry joined us at the marina Sunday morning at about 9:30. We spent some time visiting on the boat, then they took us out for brunch in Historic Yorktown. We went for a drive on Colonial Parkway, through Historic Williamsburg, and to Karen's new townhouse in Williamsburg, where we met her 20-year old son Charlie. From there, we all went over to Diane and Terry's new house, just five minutes away. Both families moved up to Williamsburg from Yorktown in May/June to be closer to Terry's office and their kids.

We spent a very pleasant day with them and Diane and Terry's son Alex, who is 21, their daughter Steph, son-in-law Dave, and Steph and Dave's lively, adorable 14-month old twins, Hannah and Jack.

Diane and Terry insisted that Wayne and I take their car for two days. It was such a generous offer and how could we possibly turn it down? I doubt that a newly licensed 16-year old on her first night out with the family car could have been more eager.

Monday we had 500-hour engine maintenance and other miscellaneous stuff done on the boat, then used the car for a few errands. Tuesday Wayne and I drove to Historic Williamsburg and spent most of the day exploring and imagining what it must have been like in colonial times. It was interesting, informative, and made that period of American history come alive for us. To quote from their website (www.history.org):

"In Colonial Williamsburg's 301-acre Historic Area stand hundreds of restored, reconstructed, and historically furnished buildings. Costumed interpreters tell the stories of the men and women of the 18th-century city—black, white, and native

American, slave, indentured, and free—and the challenges they faced. In this historic place, we help the future learn from the past."

Later . . . Diane called me this morning at 9:00 to see if we had time for visitors before heading to Norfolk. Diane and Karen's other sister Marilyn and her husband Paul were visiting from Minnesota and wanted to drive down and see us and the boat. We did not want to pass up the opportunity, so we moved our departure time back a bit and welcomed them aboard for a quick but pleasant visit.

Everyone wants to live on top of the mountain,
but all the happiness and growth
occurs while you're climbing it.

~ *Andy Rooney*

Chapter 7

© 2012 Google

Intracoastal Waterway from Norfolk to Miami

October 18 - November 8

163

We cannot direct the wind,
but we can adjust the sails.

~ *Bertha Calloway*

Thursday, October 18, 2007:

Awesome warships in Norfolk, Virginia

As we were leaving the York River yesterday, Al and Betsy on *Morning Star* (another Island Packet) saw *Lena Bea* and hailed us on the VHF radio. They're from Virginia and have been following our blog, which they learned about from the Island Packet email list! Hi, Al and Betsy! Wish we could have met you in person and are pleased to hear that you're enjoying our blog.

Now we're docked at Waterside Marina in downtown Norfolk for two nights. We may stay longer, but there's a big wine festival on the waterfront this weekend and the marina will be full with prior reservations (dang . . . wish we'd known about that earlier . . . and for more than one reason). We'll try to anchor nearby if we decide to stay longer.

Regardless of how you feel about the war, it was a jaw-dropping experience to cruise through Norfolk and see all the "warships," as they are called. There were dozens of them and they made us feel like an insignificant speck on the water. It was interesting to listen to them on the VHF radio; we heard one ship—"amphibious assault ship number seven"—announce that he was under way just moments before we saw him leave the dock.

I am not interested in warships (or ships of any kind, really), but even I was impressed. Just one look at these intimidating monsters should be enough to make the enemy surrender.

Friday, October 19, 2007:

Freaked-out captain

We are about to leave Norfolk and Wayne seems on the verge of a nervous breakdown. We will, God willing, pass under the first of some 65-foot bridges today, and Wayne is calling everyone from the Army Corps of Engineers to the Coast Guard to President Bush (okay, probably not him) to find out if it is truly 65 feet, or, as we have read, possibly a foot or two lower. Our mast is supposedly 62 feet—we have not measured it—but if you add on the VHF antenna and the anemometer (wind instrument), it's probably 63 feet, give or take a few inches. Sure wish I had some tranquilizers for the captain. Stay tuned . . . Meanwhile, your prayers will be greatly appreciated.

Saturday, October 20, 2007:

"Me" time and the first of many bridges

Friday, October 19 – When I found out there was an actual shopping mall within walking distance of the marina, I knew how I would spend our first day in Norfolk. I needed to get some exercise and some alone time. Wayne had boat projects to do, which invariably involves removing all the cushions from the settees so he can get to the areas he needs to work in, and having tools, cushions, and junk scattered all over the boat. The chaos makes me a wee bit crazy since there's usually no place left to sit, I'm in his way, and it can be hazardous trying to step around tools and whatnot. He was probably glad to have a little space himself, so it was a win-win deal.

[Men will probably want to skip this paragraph.] I was at the mall ten minutes before it opened, pacing in front of the Dillard's entrance, looking at my watch every thirty seconds. I think the last time I was at an actual shopping mall was in Sault Sainte Marie, and that was rushed. I did not intend to buy anything, but having time to just browse as long as I wanted was a luxury; I spent five hours there! Speaking of luxury, the first thing I did was treat myself to a badly needed (and well deserved) pedicure. Aaaaaah! As I told Wayne afterwards, I finally felt feminine again; I have not worn any makeup since well before the start of our trip and the pedicure was a luxurious indulgence.

The marina couldn't let us stay another night because of the wine festival this weekend, and all of the anchorages nearby appeared to be fully occupied. We had wanted to see Nauticus (The National Maritime Center), which is now the permanent home of the largest U.S. battleship ever constructed, the *USS Wisconsin*. There was no time to tour Nauticus, but we did run over to tour the *USS Wisconsin* before checkout time at noon.

Although mile "0" on the Intracoastal Waterway is in Norfolk, the ICW actually starts in Boston (some resources say Maine, and yes, it does include the Chesapeake Bay). From Boston it goes south to Florida and then along the Gulf Coast to the Mexican border, through interconnected canals, creeks, rivers, bays, and sounds. In Punta Gorda, Florida, it goes through a large body of water, Charlotte Harbor, and is marked with buoys.

We started this section of the Intracoastal Waterway in the Virginia Cut, which feels like a river (sometimes a creek) lined with forests, grasses, and marshes, and traversed by many bridges. We passed through one lock and under three lift bridges, five bascule bridges, and three swing bridges. A few are open continuously except when needed by a passing train, but most of them only open on the hour and the half hour, and some don't open at all between 7-9 a.m. and 4-6 p.m. due to rush hour traffic. There were also two fixed bridges, each with 65 feet of vertical clearance.

At Wayne's insistence I stood on the bow trying to calculate whether or not we would make it under the first fixed bridge, and make it we did (Hallelujah!), with probably a couple of feet to spare. As I returned to the cockpit, Wayne asked if I would steer while he went down to change his pants.

The second fixed bridge was a different story: we cleared it, but barely. From my vantage point on the bow, there did not appear to be any space between the anemometer and the bridge; we think the antenna hit it.

Yikes! I just looked at the chart and counted thirteen 65-foot bridges (one is 64 feet) ahead of us in North Carolina alone! I told Wayne and he said we will probably go out in the Atlantic to avoid some of them.

We took a slip at the Pungo Ferry Marina for the night.

Remember how far you've come,
not just how far you have to go.

~ *Rick Warren*

Sunday, October 21, 2007:

Faith or folly?

Faith: \fāth\ (1): firm belief in something for which there is no proof (2): complete trust (3): to pass under a bridge said to have vertical clearance of 64 feet in a boat approximated to be 63 feet high.

Saturday, October 20 – We anchored at the mouth of the Alligator River in North Carolina after a day of spectacular sailing through the Albemarle Sound. We made it safely under two more 65-foot bridges without incident, but not without anxiety.

Sunday, October 21 – Wayne is starting to feel so comfortable with these bridges that he asked me to take photos as we passed under a few today. The water depth under some of them can vary by as much as two feet, depending on tide and wind, so we approached the 64-foot bridge with apprehension, especially after seeing this ambiguous sign:

We anchored at Belhaven, NC and dinghied into shore. A quick look around town revealed that nothing appeared to be open nearby except the local Ace Hardware store. Very interesting place. They sell everything from the usual hardware fare to clothing, used books, kitchen appliances, and wine. There was even a cooler filled with beer, champagne, caviar, fresh crabmeat, and gourmet cheeses . . . on the same shelf as the boxes of NIGHT CRAWLERS!

~~~~

Monday, October 22, 2007:

Change of plans . . . again

Yesterday and today we have been in the company of many more sailboats than we were over the weekend—fellow cruisers heading for Florida, the Bahamas, the Caribbean, and other points south. Much of the channel through this part of the Intracoastal Waterway is so narrow—not unlike a two-lane road—that boats will radio each other if they want to pass, so the increase in traffic definitely has an impact.

Last week we got word from our insurance company, which has had the policy of making absolutely no exceptions in this regard, that they have given us the go-ahead to travel south of 35 degrees latitude before November 1. Yesterday we were en route to Oriental, North Carolina, to get the official approval, but Wayne was able to talk to the insurance folks by cell phone and get the written confirmation by satellite phone and email while underway. Don't you love it when technology works? This affects our plans in a big way: instead of traveling nonstop from Oriental, NC to Miami, we have time to stop in Charleston, South Carolina, and Savannah, Georgia.

I may have already mentioned this (it's hard to remember what I've said in the blog and what I have only said in emails), but we have a deadline of making it to Punta Gorda, Florida, before Thanksgiving on November 22 because two of our kids (Michael and Suzanne) and their families and our moms are coming to visit. I want to get there the weekend before Thanksgiving at the latest to allow us time to unpack, regroup, catch our breath, and get the house opened up and ready for company. Being able to head south earlier should allow us more than enough time.

A big disappointment in North Carolina is that we are not able to go to the Outer Banks because of shallow water. With that in mind, we decided to skip a planned stop in Oriental ("The Sailing Capital of North Carolina"), and go all the way to Beaufort, North Carolina, tonight. From there we can take a water taxi to Shackleford Banks and Cape Lookout, which will give us a small taste of the Outer Banks. When we depart

Beaufort on Wednesday, we will leave the Intracoastal Waterway (weather permitting) and sail the Atlantic to the Cape Fear Inlet, which returns us to the ICW.

We plan to arrive in Charleston Friday or Saturday; the best part is that my mom and her friend Mary are planning to

Out for a swim with the kids

drive up from Winter Haven, Florida, to visit us for a couple of days! We are so excited about that. (You can't back out now, Mom—it's on the blog.) Gary DeSantis (friend of Wayne's and the Is-land Packet dealer we bought our boat from) plans to join us in Charleston, too, and will probably sail all the way to Miami with us.

Disclaimer: all plans are subject to change based on weather, winds, and whatnot, including the whims of captain and crew.

Monday, October 22, 2007:

Uh-oh! Not again!

We were twenty minutes from Beaufort, North Carolina, and I was taking a quick shower when all of a sudden, thud! The boat stopped abruptly and the first thought that came to mind was, *Why did he slam on the brakes?* HA! The second thought was, *Oh. The boat doesn't have any brakes. So what made it stop so abruptly?* I grabbed a towel and ran to see what was going on, only to find a very irate captain who had just run aground. Again. I shrugged my shoulders and said, "Just call TowBoatUS." Wayne did not appreciate the suggestion, so I made myself scarce while he figured out what to do. Before long I felt us moving again. He had wiggled and finessed the boat free with the help of the engine and the rising tide. However, because of the shallow water, we were forced to take a detour of an hour and a half to get to the Beaufort Docks Marina, where we docked for two nights.

Tuesday, October 23, 2007:

ICW, bridges, and schedules

"Wayne again. Of course, each time I go to write something Michele has beat me to it, but I thought I would add a few thoughts anyway.

"So far we have traveled about 200 nautical miles in the Intracoastal Waterway since leaving Norfolk. I had hoped to avoid some of the ICW by going outside in the Atlantic. By going outside, I can avoid bridges and shoals. Shoals are submerged sand bars that shift with the currents, and reduced funds for dredging has made the problem much worse in the last several years. The soft grounding Michele referred to on Monday was caused by shoaling. I had turned away from the sand bar and slowed down as the depth quickly dropped, but I still caught the edge, which is why we were lucky enough to get off with a little help from a rising tidal current.

"As far as going outside (in the Atlantic), sometimes that option gives us a shorter distance and we are able to go faster. Of course, going outside has its own set of problems, the primary one being weather, so I have to constantly look at the pros and cons. I was hoping to go outside tomorrow to save time, but the weather is not cooperating, so we will take the ICW.

"About those bridges! They have been a concern since before we left the marina in Bayfield. It's very scary to go under a bridge that is only one or two feet taller than your mast. It appears that you're going to hit the bridge until you are under it. I also have to avoid hitting the navigation lights that usually hang down from the bridge, and I need to watch tide levels and currents. It is much easier now that we have gone under several of them, but I will still approach the bridges with caution!"

Tuesday, October 23, 2007:

Yet another tragedy

Our son Joey called us on Monday with tragic news: Jeremy, a friend of Joey and his roommate, lost his mom and brother—his only parent and only sibling—in a car crash. Jayson's friend Nicholle was also killed. Please remember

Jeremy in your prayers, and also ask God to show Joey and Kyle how they can best support their friend during this unspeakably tragic time.

Thursday, October 25, 2007:

Variety and vigilance on the ICW

For the most part, we have found it a pleasure to cruise the Intracoastal Waterway; the scenery is lovely and it is far more interesting than sailing in the Atlantic, miles from shore. We are seeing more wildlife, too: the first dolphins since Canada, many birds, and today we even saw a bunch of goats. There's evidence that we are farther south, including palm trees (In North Carolina? That's pushing it.), the first pelicans of the trip, and yes, even no-see-ums.

It's slow-going on the ICW, though, and requires vigilance. With shallow water due to shoaling in many places, we often have to slow down; we scraped bottom a couple of times and came close several more times today. Because of that, it is easier and more relaxing to travel during  high tide, but it's less stressful going under bridges at low tide. I must say, though, that the bridges have almost become a non-issue; we have gone under so many that we've gotten used to them, and of course it helps that we have not hit one (yet).

The weather continues to be hot and muggy and cools off very little at night, but we don't complain, considering what the weather could be in the heart of hurricane season. Today we were supposed to be in thunderstorms all day and they  totally missed us; more are predicted for tomorrow.

Because the ICW is so narrow and shallow (so far, anyway), there are very few places to anchor, but last night we had planned to anchor in Calabash Creek in Little River, South Carolina, which someone had told us is a very pleasant anchorage. Well, we tried to get into the creek but ran aground at the entrance. (How did all those other boats get in there?) Wayne managed to get us free and was not about to try again, so we ended up at Harbour Village Marina in Hampstead.

It annoys me to have to dock when we would rather anchor and then have to pay for it besides. Many of these marinas have wonderful facilities, which mariners pay for whether they  use them or not, and we do not. All we need is a place to tie up the boat so we can sleep. It's like being on a road trip and staying at a Marriott when all you want or need is a bed and a shower. Or traveling in an RV and being forced to pay for a campground with all the amenities when all you need is a truck stop or Walmart parking lot so you can catch a few winks. Tonight's accommodations at the Coquina Yacht Club in Little River, South Carolina, are a bargain, though, at only $1.00/foot ($45).

Friday, October 26, 2007:

God's protection

"I think you scraped some paint off your mast on that one, Captain," were the words radioed to us by the captain of the boat behind us, referring to the first of a set of three fixed bridges we slipped under. Although we're watching, it is impossible to tell whether we're going to make it or not until we are clear, yet Wayne expects me to watch from the bow and give him a confident thumbs up or down. This was one of the worst so far. It did not appear that we could clear it, but we did. Whew! All things considered, a little paint is a small sacrifice to make.

Although radar showed that we were surrounded by thunderstorms today, we only experienced periodic light showers (excluding the heavy downpour that delayed our departure by half an hour). We were grateful to have missed the storm that left trees standing in water and the Waterway littered with leaves and branches.

Inadequate depth was almost not an issue today. Our shallow-water alarm, which we have set to go off at eight feet, didn't go off until the last hour of the day, and even then the water didn't get terribly shallow. We did get stuck while anchoring in Five Fathom Creek, but the rising tide freed us within minutes.

We were awakened before dawn by a fleet of shrimp boats heading out for the day. It was tight quarters in the narrow creek and they probably weren't happy about us obstructing their passageway.

Saturday, October 27, 2007:

I get to see my mom!

Today we'll be docking in Charleston, South Carolina, where we have a busy weekend planned. Mom and her friend Mary are coming to Charleston today and will be staying with us until Tuesday; we plan to do some sightseeing. Gary DeSantis will join us on Sunday and stay to accompany us on the next leg of our journey.

Today is notable for another reason: three months ago, on July 27, we left the dock in Bayfield, Wisconsin. Wow. Sometimes I can hardly believe we've really done this and made it so far. Yesterday I packed up our down, fleece, and woolens to send back with Mom. We're on the home stretch and it feels *good*.

Tuesday, October 30, 2007:

Charleston and a mega yacht tour

Tuesday, October 30 – We're at the Charleston City Marina, home of the Megadock. They provide a service we haven't seen before: a free *USA Today* newspaper delivered to the boat each morning—first newspapers I've read since leaving home three months ago, and I've always been a daily newspaper reader.

Mom and Mary arrived around dinnertime on Saturday and the four of us decided to go out. As we left, we stopped to gawk at a magnificent yacht that was docked in front of us. We were peering into the engine room, the only area we could see into, when a guy standing nearby commented that not too many women are so interested in seeing engine rooms. I replied that we were only looking in the engine room because we couldn't see the galley, to which he responded, "Would you like to see the galley?" We enthusiastically accepted his offer, so he brought us inside and gave us a tour of this beauty, one of the 100 largest yachts in America and worth 21 million. She is grand, plush, and opulent, and appears to lack nothing you would expect to find in a multimillion dollar house (as if I would know). She took our breath away: marble floors, exquisitely carved ceilings, beautiful exotic woods, priceless art. She has four guest cabins and five crew cabins. The luxurious owner's stateroom includes his and her bathrooms with a jacuzzi. The galley (there's a separate galley downstairs for the crew) is all stainless steel, including the walls, and has everything you could possibly expect to see on the wish list of the most demanding professional chef.

The owner of the yacht does not travel on it—the crew brings it to wherever he wants to go and he flies to that location. Every time it's moved, of course, everything inside the yacht must be secured and all the valuable artwork gets carefully wrapped and packed away. (On our boat, the biggest concern is to secure the coffee maker.)

The full-time crew of seven sign confidentiality agreements and aren't even allowed to say who owns her, but with a little internet sleuthing, I was able to find out on my own. Sorry, but I can't tell . . . don't want to get our tour guide fired.

The rest of the weekend was fun, if anticlimactic. On Sunday, Mom, Mary, Wayne, and I took a mini bus tour of

Charleston—a beautifully preserved and restored historic city. Gary flew in on Sunday afternoon. This was the first time we've had more than one extra person spend the night on the boat. We can accommodate seven people comfortably . . . as long as no one brings any stuff and doesn't walk around *(Lena Bea* ain't no mega yacht). It might have been a little too claustrophobic

for Mom and Mary, because they decided to leave Monday morning instead of Tuesday. They said it was because they wanted to stop and see a little of Savannah on the way home.

I spent the afternoon strolling around downtown Charleston, while Wayne and Gary perused the Maritime Museum. They stopped and picked up some fresh salmon, which Gary prepared for dinner. It was magnifique!

We're spending the night in Beaufort, South Carolina, at Port Royal Landing Marina. We plan to leave the ICW tomorrow at 3:30-4:00 a.m. for the open waters of the Atlantic and sail to St. Simons Island in Georgia. Because there's been no funding in recent years for maintenance dredging of the ICW from south of Port Royal Sound, SC, to Cumberland Sound, GA, there are many trouble spots. Add to that a tidal range of 8-9 feet and the advice of locals to avoid the ICW in that area . . . well, it didn't take much to convince us. Of course, we checked the weather carefully before making our decision and have noted places where we can easily return to the ICW if conditions outside are unfavorable. We are keeping a close eye on the tropical storm, Noel. I'm disappointed that this means missing a stopover in Savannah, but we have to weigh our options and make the best decision based on all factors, safety being primary.

This afternoon we knew we would miss the final opening of a swing bridge that is closed between 4-6 p.m. to recreational traffic. Just as we resigned ourselves to waiting it out for two hours, we noticed a tugboat coming up behind us pushing a barge. The bridge opens for tugboats, so Wayne sped up and stayed with him. He then radioed the bridge and they allowed us to slip through behind the tug at 5:00.

Thursday, November 1, 2007:

A rough day in the Atlantic

Wednesday, October 31 – It was one of those days when you just pray to make it to the nearest anchorage quickly and without throwing up. We avoided the hazards of the ICW in this section and made twice the distance (101 nautical miles) we would have otherwise, but it wasn't a freebie. Winds from the north-northeast at 25-30 knots with waves as high as fourteen feet in the Atlantic left us all feeling green around the gills, especially Gary, who was just starting to find his sea legs. He and I tried to sleep as much as we could, which is about all you can do to get through it.

We left the marina at 4 a.m. I went around and made sure everything was secure, then did it again after we were out in open water and the second tier of stuff went flying around the cabin. However, today was a three-tier day: items that were safely stashed behind the settees in the salon forced cushions out of the way to emerge from their hiding places.

With Gary (a very experienced sailor) aboard, they didn't really need me, so I was able to take care of myself. Trying to sleep in the cockpit would have been impossible because it was so rough, so I went downstairs. To keep from rolling, I laid across the mattress at the head of the bed with pillows between me and the cabin wall to cushion myself from being thrown against it. On my other side, I put a rolled-up quilt stuffed with pillows. It was still hard to sleep, but at least I was *relatively* safe and comfortable.

I don't think any of us saw a single other boat out there; few boats can handle the conditions we had, and there are, arguably, none better than the Island Packet.

We anchored off St. Simon's Island, Georgia, at 5:15, after what may have been the longest thirteen hours of my life. We had an early dinner and were all in bed by 8:00.

It feels good to be in the calm and security of the ICW again today, and the view is better, too.

QUESTION OF THE DAY: "What does it mean, to get your 'sea legs?'"

Answer: *The term refers to how the body adjusts to the motion of a boat, i.e., the ability to walk steadily and maintain balance on the deck of a boat and avoid seasickness. The body adjusts more quickly for someone who is used to being on a boat. "Sea legs" is also used as a metaphor for adjusting to life or travel at sea.*

Through many dangers, toils and snares,
I have already come; 'Tis grace has brought me
safe thus far, And grace will lead me home.

~ *John Newton*

183

Thursday, November 1, 2007:

Slow day waiting for bridges and tides

Message from Captain Wayne: "Well, after a great day in the Atlantic yesterday, or at least a day where we covered considerable distance, today we only made 48 nautical miles instead of the planned 69. We started out making great time. With 15-25-knot winds, we were sailing down the ICW at over eight knots most of the day, so we expected to easily arrive at Jacksonville Beach by 3 p.m.

"If you guessed our delay was due to bridges again, you are correct. We arrived at the Seaboard System Railroad Swing Bridge about 2:15 p.m. The bridge is normally open, but a train was coming, so we had to wait about twenty minutes in strong wind and currents until the train passed and the bridge was slowly opened. This bridge is immediately followed by a pair of 65-foot twin fixed bridges.

"Because it was nearly high tide, with higher than normal high tides due to the lunar cycle and strong current, I was especially concerned, so it was all hands on deck to see if we could clear. An Island Packet 440 with the same mast height arrived just behind us with the same concerns. They were glad they could watch us to see if we made it before trying it themselves.

"When we approach a fixed bridge we always look for a tide board, which tells us the height of the bridge based on current water level. We didn't see one at the A1A bridge. After going through the swing bridge and slowing the boat as much as I could against a following current and twenty-knot winds, I noticed the tide board on the right side of the A1A fixed bridge angled in such a way that you had to be almost beside it to read it. The tide board showed 62 feet, which is eighteen inches less than needed for us to pass under the bridge. I scrambled to turn around in the narrow channel while warning the other boat that there was not enough clearance. Fortunately, I was able to stop and turn around less than thirty feet from the bridge. I am sure glad that *Lena Bea* has bow thrusters, a feathering propeller, and a powerful engine to be able to turn around in a 1.7 knot current with following winds of 18-22 knots.

"After making our U-turn, we anchored to wait for the tide—and our heart rates—to go down. I calculated that the tide wouldn't allow us to clear the bridge until about 5:10 p.m. We passed under at 5:20 with only an inch or two to spare (we think the antenna may have ticked against the bottom of the support beams), three hours after we arrived! The delay meant that we wouldn't be able to make it to Jacksonville Beach. We found a great place to anchor about five miles after the bridge (near marker 36 at Amelia City), but we won't be able to get to St. Augustine as early as we had hoped for tomorrow.

"So cruising goes on the ICW. At least our mast is undamaged and we are securely anchored. Michele made a wonderful dinner again tonight, and now we can relax and plan the next segment of our trip. Weather is keeping us in the ICW for at least another couple of days, and we are glad that Hurricane Noel is continuing the projected path to the Northeast. I get real time information through Sirius and can track it on our Raymarine E80 displays."

Friday, November 2, 2007:

Setting the record straight

I received an interesting email from a friend commenting on Wayne's post from yesterday. Here is an excerpt: " . . . A fascinating juxtaposition of your blog from the day before and his today. You wrote of the tumult and Wayne begins simply 'Well after a great day in the Atlantic . . .' What a contrast! When I finished your blog with the image of you curled up on your bed and Gary off somewhere fighting being green, I wondered how the captain fared. I learned today in his blog and clearly he fared well . . . "

All three of us roared with laughter when I read aloud Tim's misconception about the captain faring well. There's no way Gary and I are about to let Wayne get away with leaving that impression, so here he is with clarification:

Captain Wayne: "Oops! I was laughing as well! The 'great day' in my post was referring only to the distance we covered that day. The ride was as uncomfortable as any I have been on. The waves were steep and coming from several directions, sort of piling into heaps most of the day. Gary called them 'hay stackers,' which is a great description. The wind was so close off the stern that sails did not help the motion. At least we were safe and secure in our Island Packet, even if we were ALL a little green."

QUESTION OF THE DAY (oh, go on, admit you were wondering the same things): "What's it like to use the toilet facilities when the boat is always in motion, and for that matter, what it is like to take a shower in those conditions?"

Answer: *First the easy one. There is a place to sit in the shower and I brace my feet against the wall (a small shower can be a blessing). The shower head is on a hose and can be taken from its bracket on the wall to use by hand. I spray myself, put the shower down, soap and shampoo, pick up the shower, and rinse—using only one hand for the whole procedure, as the other is always hanging on to something. Wayne has never had to do this, and trust me, there are days when I'd sooner jump overboard than try to take a shower.*

Other feats are not as easily avoided, and that brings me back to your first question, which I will attempt to answer delicately: The motion isn't usually a problem unless there is too much of it. In those conditions, when one is seated, one generally braces oneself with both feet against the cabinet and grabs hold of whatever one can to keep from falling off. It's not easy to pull one's pants up or down when one needs both hands to hang on for dear life. On more than one occasion I have returned from a trip to the head and grumbled to Wayne, "I wish I were a guy."

Now, aren't you glad you asked?

Saturday, November 3, 2007:

Florida at last!

What a jubilant feeling it was to sail across the Florida state line on November 1! In the back of my mind it has been my target date, and even though we weren't specifically shooting for it, we were right on. We're definitely on the home stretch now, and should easily make it to Punta Gorda by the 15th, if not sooner.

We're seeing many dolphins, which never cease to delight us, and signs warning boaters of manatees have become common. If someone had blindfolded us and dropped us off here, we would have known we were in Florida because of the tropical vegetation and the home styles with pool cages and tile roofs. There is significantly more pleasure-boat traffic, and power boaters here aren't as courteous—many roar by without warning and without slowing down, leaving us to rock wildly in their wakes. In the Carolinas and Georgia, mariners usually radioed us to state their intentions or ask permission to pass, and then promised (and kindly gave us) a "slow" or "gentle" pass. Many do here as well, but we can't depend on it. It especially disturbs me to see so many power boaters ignore the manatee zone signs.

Although Hurricane Noel started out on Friday directly east of us and a little over 400 miles away, the effect on us in the ICW was negligible. Had we been in the Atlantic, we'd probably have a story to tell that would make Wednesday sound like a walk on the beach. Sorry to disappoint you, I know you would have enjoyed the excitement.

If the insurance company had not given us the go ahead to travel south of Cape Hatteras before November 1, we'd probably be hunkering down for a couple of days, partly because strong wind and waves would have made going under all those bridges much more treacherous. Looking at where Noel has been and where he's headed, where we've been and where we could be now, we have no doubt that God continues to protect us. For that and for who He is, we give God thanks and praise.

Friday we anchored off Amelia City, Florida. Yesterday we docked at Camachee Cove Yacht Harbor in St. Augustine and borrowed the marina's courtesy car for a quick self-guided tour of the city. We parked the car and strolled the narrow, old, cobblestone streets lined with old Spanish architecture. St. Augustine was founded in 1565 as a Spanish military outpost and is the oldest continuously occupied European settlement in the United States. Traces of the city's Spanish heritage are everywhere, and we were taken with its charm. We only had a couple of hours, unfortunately, because we had to return the car. Gary treated us to a wonderful dinner at the marina, then went for a run and returned to the little city to find it hopping with nightlife.

We received an email from Rachael and Claus on November 5: "Hey you two Floridians! Congratulations on making it to Florida in record time and avoiding Noel! It looks like you'll be all settled in by the time your family arrives for Thanksgiving!

"We finally made it to Annapolis! We're renting a car tomorrow and going to visit some of my relatives in the DC area. That will be fun, but it's getting cold again and time to get farther south. We won't be sitting around the Chesapeake much; just making our way through and seeing what we can.

"Claus measured the mast today in preparation for the ICW—58 feet, just like we thought. Now we can worry about the depth. Enjoy the last leg of your trip. We miss you!"

Wednesday, November 7, 2007:

Catching up and What's for dinner?

Wednesday, November 7 – Our cruise down the East Coast of Florida has been a pleasure, and if you're wondering why you haven't heard from me, it's because I've been delighting in the sights, the beautiful weather, clear blue skies, dolphins frolicking alongside the boat, and an occasional manatee sighting. Now we're approaching Miami Beach. Here's a brief rundown of the past few days:

On Saturday we traveled the ICW from St. Augustine to Daytona Beach, where we anchored for the night. Sunday and Monday nights we docked at Melbourne Harbor Marina. We rented a car there and drove up to the Kennedy Space

Center for the day. It surpassed our expectations and we were all glad we took the time to visit it.

En route to the Space Center, we traveled over a bridge that we had traveled under the previous day, which is notable because our antenna went plink, plink, plink, as it hit the support beams of the bridge passing through.

We've been traveling on and off with another Island Packet, *Gigi*, and together we've braved the bridges, sometimes taking turns at being the first to pass under. We've had some very close calls, including one yesterday where we *backed* under the bridge so we could extricate ourselves more easily if it looked as if the anemometer would hit. The flexible antenna of about eighteen inches bent in half as it hit the support beams, but the anemometer was clear.

If you're sick of hearing about bridges, imagine how sick we are of negotiating them.

We've been able to sail with the genoa quite a bit in the

ICW. Gary is a very experienced sailor, and by his account, 99% of his experience has been racing. It doesn't matter that there's no one to race with—Gary reminds me of a race horse that just has to do what it was bred to do, so if the sails are up, Gary is constantly trimming them to maximize speed. I told him we would have been in Punta Gorda weeks ago if he had been with us the whole trip. It's been fun having him aboard.

Yesterday we left the confines of the ICW for the blue waters of the Atlantic so we could fly our spinnaker and avoid numerous bridges. Surprisingly, there are very few safe inlets for passing between the ICW and the ocean because of shoaling and other hazards, and we would have gone outside sooner had there been the opportunity. There wasn't much wind, but we definitely made the most of what we had. It was much more pleasant than our day in the Atlantic last week.

As much as I like to sleep with a little wave action, last night's anchorage (in the ocean, about half a mile off Jupiter Island beach) wasn't much fun. There was way too much rolling with the waves hitting us from the side, and that made dinner preparation a worse chore than normal, even though I only needed to heat things up. Sleep was another challenge, and I don't think the three of us got a combined total of eight hours. We decided not to fight it, and pulled up the anchor at about 3:30; Gary and I were able to go down and catch a few more hours of sleep once we were underway.

QUESTION OF THE DAY: "What do you eat and how do you prepare meals while underway?"

Answer: *For breakfast, we'll usually grab a bowl of cereal with frozen berries or fresh fruit, if we have it. We always have* milk on hand, and the powdered kind is convenient and easy to store. We've also used the shelf-stable milk that comes in one-quart cartons, but it's more expensive and adds bulk and weight.

For lunch, Wayne will eat a sandwich or open a can [or more recently, packet] of sardines, salmon, or tuna to eat on crackers. I'll usually have a protein shake. Hard-boiled eggs are a convenient and nutritious staple, and we often snack on nuts, fruit, or cheese and crackers.

We are extremely fortunate to have a microwave oven, a large freezer, and storage space galore, so dinner isn't much different from how we eat at home, except there's less fresh produce. Before we left, I made large batches of red and white chili and soups, which I froze in individual serving sizes. I baked meatloaves and sliced them before freezing so we can take out a slice or two as needed. Of course, we have pasta, frozen steaks, boneless and skinless chicken pieces, burgers, and so on. We like brown and wild rice mixed together for a side dish, but they take up to an hour to cook, so I even cooked and froze those in Ziplocks before our trip. We don't eat many processed foods, such as boxed pasta or rice entrees, but have included canned fruits, vegetables, and soups on this trip out of necessity.

I strongly prefer not to cook while we're underway, but sometimes it's unavoidable. We have a gimbaled propane stove (standard equipment on most boats) which pivots as the boat moves to keep the stove level and pans from sliding off the burners. I rely a lot on my microwave, but sometimes the boat is heeling (leaning over) too much and liquid-y foods, such as soup, would tend to spill. I learned to use a pressure cooker, an essential piece of equipment on many boats. It saves much time and propane, and I should probably use it more than I do. We also have a small propane grill.

If we know ahead of time that the conditions will be rough, I'll make sandwiches or something in the morning to grab when we're hungry so I can avoid being in the cabin more than necessary.

[We've made a few changes in our menus since this trip. Now we'll usually have a homemade breakfast bar with our morning coffee. I learned how to make Greek yogurt with no special equipment, and always have it in the refrigerator, both at home and on the boat. Wayne enjoys it with frozen blueberries and Kashi cereal, while I prefer to add the yogurt and blueberries to my protein shake.

Before we cruised to the Bahamas the first time, we learned that it can be hard to find bread down in the Exumas so I bake all our bread. Indeed, we found that finding groceries of any description down there was uncertain, depending on when the supply boat last made a delivery, and everything is expensive. Because of that, I provision for the entire trip when we go to the Exumas—two months worth—but pick up fresh produce when it's available.]

It's 1:40 p.m. and we just docked at South Beach, so please excuse me while I grab my bikini . . .

Thursday, November 8, 2007:

Joe's Stone Crab, South Beach

The three of us decided days ago that dinner in Miami had to be at Joe's Stone Crab (not to be confused with Joe's Crab Shack), as we all had delectable memories of it from previous visits, so it wasn't

by accident that we chose to dock at Miami Beach Marina, a block away. We knew it was a splurge (the marina as well as the dinner), but justified it by saying it was our last dinner together, and probably Wayne's and my last restaurant meal of the trip, as well. Joe's fully met our expectations.

The realization has hit me! No more restaurants . . . no more provisioning . . . no more doing laundry at marinas . . . no more refueling . . . no more water tank refills . . . no more pump outs . . . Wow! We're almost home, less than a week away (three hours by car, but I don't let myself think about that)! When I think back over the past three-and-a-half months, it almost seems like a dream. Did we *really* do all that? Well over 4000 nautical miles traveled and less than 300 to go. Unbelievable!

Gary just left and it was sad to see him go—he's a great guy and we enjoyed his company. I know that Wayne appreciated having a good guy friend aboard for a while, especially a fellow sailing

enthusiast who knows and appreciates an Island Packet as much as he does.

Chapter 8

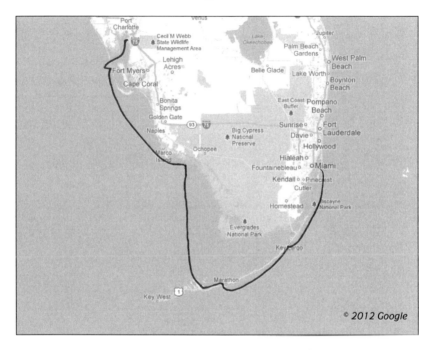

© 2012 Google

Miami to
Punta Gorda

November 8 - November 12

We need to find God, and he cannot be found in noise and restlessness. God is the friend of silence. See how nature— trees, flowers, grass—grows in silence; see the stars, the moon and the sun, how they move in silence...

~ *Mother Teresa*

Sunday, November 11, 2007:

Plowing a channel through the Keys

We left Miami Beach around noon on Thursday, sailed 51 nautical miles in the Atlantic to Hawk Channel, and anchored south of Key Largo. Friday brought us 74 nautical miles closer to home with another day of perfect sailing south of the Keys. We aborted an intended Saturday layover in Key West when I phoned the local marinas for reservations and learned from the third one I called that they were all full due to a big power boat race this weekend. We were happy to know about that in advance so we could avoid it. Instead, we went to Plan B: rather than continuing on the outside south of the Keys and around the west side of Key West (35 nautical miles farther, but a safer passage due to deeper water), we passed north through Moser Channel and under Seven Mile Bridge to Big Spanish Channel, and found a place to anchor near Little Pine Key.

How does a boat with a five-foot draft not run aground in water that is 3½-4 feet deep? That is the question I kept asking myself Saturday morning as I stood on the bowsprit in a futile attempt to guide Wayne through the "deeper" water, which in reality was "extremely shallow" and "shallower still." I'm 5'2½" and the water could not have been more than waist deep in places. A couple of weeks ago, Wayne measured around the boat with a portable depth sounder to determine how much our depth instrument varied from the actual depth of the water. He found that the instruments give a reading one foot less than the actual depth—a good thing. Considering that, we were still in 3½-4 foot-deep water with our five-foot draft, somehow plowing our way through the sand or whatever it was on the bottom. It obviously wasn't coral, I did not see weeds, and Wayne swears it couldn't have been sand because we would have been stuck in it, but what else could it be? Divine intervention? Very strange.

Monday, November 12, 2007:

On the home stretch!

We haven't had internet access since leaving Miami on Thursday, so you may be surprised to hear that, as I write this on Sunday morning, we're approximately 26 hours from docking behind our house in Punta Gorda. Skipping that layover in Key West brought us one day closer to home. We anchored about five miles southwest of Indian Pass near Everglades City last night; we just passed Naples and expect to anchor off Useppa Island or Cayo Costa tonight. From there we're about four hours from home, but we promised Mom, who wants to be waiting on the dock when we come down the canal, not to arrive before she gets there, around 12:30-1:00. She helps teach a line dance class Monday morning, and with the two hour drive, can't get there before then. No problem, Mom . . . after 3½ months, we can sleep in a little on our last day and take our time.

The journey isn't done, though, and we'll have more to say when it is, so don't leave us yet.

We've had our best and longest stretch of fabulous sailing of the trip since leaving Miami; we've sailed every day and it's been close to perfect. Today and tomorrow promise to be the same.

I keep reflecting about this blog and how its importance to me on the trip was something I didn't anticipate. If you've ever thought about keeping a blog—or even if you haven't—I encourage you to try it. My cousin, Tracy, keeps a family blog with beautiful photos and very fine writing; I can only imagine what a precious gift it will be to her children someday.

Monday, November 12, 2007:

Magnificent final night of a most magnificent journey

One of our favorite things to do when we're in Florida is to take our little power boat, *Alexandra*, over to Cayo Costa, one of the barrier islands that separate the Gulf of Mexico from Charlotte Harbor. It's a state park, largely uninhabited, and accessible only by boat. We like it because the long, beautiful beach on the gulf side is usually almost deserted and offers great shelling. I've often longed to anchor offshore, walk the beach until sunset, spend the night, and walk it again the next morning, which isn't a practical option in our little 21-foot Hurricane.

It was so fitting then, that all factors aligned to make the Gulf side of Cayo Costa the best place for us to anchor tonight, the last night of our trip.

We anchored at around 3:30 and were headed in to shore in the dinghy (without a camera) when we suddenly found ourselves surrounded by a superpod of dolphins—far too many to count. We've never seen so many at one time before! We cut the engine and sat there watching them, certain that God had sent them to welcome us home. As we pulled the dinghy up on shore, the first thing I saw on the beach was a sand dollar, one of my favorite shells. I walked and combed the beach until sunset, when Wayne had to nearly drag me away, as always.

The two of us watched the sun disappear into the Gulf of Mexico, the last sunset of our trip, and sat in the cockpit drinking champagne and eating brie and crackers. We toasted our last night—unbelievable!—of a most magnificent journey.

Monday, November 12, 2007:

Minutes away

Here I am with up-to-the-minute, late-breaking news . . . I can't believe that in all my excitement I just missed our turn off the rim canal! I handed the helm over to Wayne and he is turning us around to bring us home. We'll be docking BEHIND OUR HOUSE within ten minutes!

As we glided through Charlotte Harbor on our approach to Ponce de Leon inlet which takes us into Punta Gorda Isles, a couple of neighbors called us and said, "Don't come in yet! The tide is too low and you'll go aground!" Hmm, let's think about that for a minute: We are half an hour away from completing a 109-day, 5000-mile trip and we're going to stop and wait who-knows-how-long for the tide to come in? I don't think so! In an act of defiance, determination, and faith, we plowed our way through the inlet, churning up the sand as we dredged our way through.

Chapter 9

photo by Norma Cavanaugh

HOME!

November 12 - November 30

Happiness cannot be traveled to, owned, earned, worn or consumed. Happiness is the spiritual experience of living every minute with love, grace, and gratitude.

~ Denis Waitley

Monday, November 12, 2007:

Home in Punta Gorda

We have the best neighbors in the world.

What a thrill it was to turn down our canal and see Mom and the neighbors (Al, Carol, Norma, Jay, Bill, Marge, Barb, and Bob) waiting for us on the dock, cameras in hand.

We were euphoric! We docked in our very tight spot behind the house with the help of Bill, Bob, and Al. Marge handed us a dozen roses and a bottle of pre-chilled champagne and they all took our pictures. We felt like celebrities.

Norma and Jay invited Mom and us, along with Bob, Barbara, and their brother-in-law Ronnie over for a delicious spaghetti dinner (Norma is Italian). After dinner, Barbara, who is a talented professional musician, entertained us as she accompanied herself on the piano. Norma and Jay sing beautifully as well, and they sang along while the rest of us feebly attempted to sing if we knew the words. It was a fabulous evening and a wonderful welcome home.

Yes, we have the best neighbors in the world.

And best Mom, too! She has always supported and encouraged me, but my adventures over the years have certainly given her a few grey hairs, and this trip was no exception. She admits to not being a writer, but wrote down some of the thoughts she had about the trip and asked me to "fix it up" for her. Here is what she had to say: "I had such mixed feelings about this trip. Of course, I was very happy for Shelley and Wayne—this was the trip of a lifetime! But as a mom, I was extremely concerned about their well-being on such a long trip, much of the time in the middle of nowhere. I worried about storms and the fact that they would be traveling in the middle of the hurricane season. I also knew I would miss them both so much!

"Along with the blog, Shelley was very good about keeping in contact by phone. When she called and told me when they would be in Charleston, I told her that was only 500 miles from me, and I couldn't wait to drive up there and see them! I was so excited! Spending that short time with them made the rest of the trip go quickly for me.

"Standing on the dock with their neighbors, waiting for their arrival, I kept thinking how great it will be to have their sailboat in their backyard in Florida. When the mast on their boat finally came into view around the corner, I could barely contain my excitement!  I was so happy and relieved to have them home!"

My dad would be celebrating his 88th birthday tomorrow. He would have been more excited and proud than anyone.

There are more posts to come as we collect our final thoughts and photos (and wits), so please check back.

≈≈≈

Thursday, November 15, 2007:

109 days and 4,630 nautical miles

Captain Wayne: "After leaving Miami, we sailed in nearly perfect conditions. Instead of the ICW, we took the Hawk Channel. It is the outside route, but still inside the reefs that are south of the Keys. We had a downwind wing-on-wing sail on the first day (genoa and main sails on opposite sides of the boat), a spinnaker run the second day, and when we headed north in the Gulf of Mexico, the wind was off the beam. What a great way to end the trip! We did take a shortcut at Marathon, going under the Seven Mile Bridge and through the Old Spanish Channel to the Gulf of Mexico.

"We covered 4,630 nautical miles (5,325 statute miles) and traveled for 109 days. We were in four Great Lakes, the St Lawrence Seaway, the Saguenay Fjord, the Gulf of St. Lawrence, the Atlantic Ocean, the Gulf of Mexico, and countless bays, rivers, lakes, channels, and canals. We negotiated eighteen locks as we descended about 900 feet from Lake Superior to sea level. We visited five Canadian provinces and eighteen U.S. states. We spent 62 nights in marinas, 34 at anchor, eight on moorings, two docked behind a friend's house, and we sailed through the night on three occasions. We spent time in about 46 different towns or cities. Last but definitely not least, we passed under 57 bridges that were 64-67 feet high.

"We met scores of interesting people and many cruisers headed to different parts of the world. Friends and family visited us along the way, and more would have joined us if we could have made our schedules work.

"We tested and refined our knowledge and skills with the boat, navigation, weather, unfamiliar waters, currents, and tides. Michele and I also worked well together as a team.

"As thrilled as we were to get home to Punta Gorda, I already miss being on *Lena Bea*, and look forward to our next voyage. I'm glad we could share our adventure with all of you. Thank you for your emails, blog comments, phone calls, and prayers.

"Stay tuned for more thoughts from Michele."

Friday, November 16, 2007:

Adjusting to life at home

We've been home four days now and are gradually getting our land legs back, both literally and figuratively. For the first few days I experienced a common phenomenon: the illusion of motion often felt by someone on dry land after spending time at sea. I also had to fight the inclination to secure things around the house so they wouldn't go flying. I kept looking at the boat docked behind the house, wondering why it looked so strange; it finally occurred to me that our home for the past 109 days was parked in the backyard of our other home. We're getting used to having "luxuries," such as a dishwasher, TV, radio, laundry facilities, a roomy shower, a king-sized bed, and as much internet access as we want. We're getting used to being more than thirty feet away from each other. It feels good to be back on land, back to our "normal" life.

I had looked forward to being able to sleep later than 6 a.m., but ironically I've been up before Wayne every day except one—wide awake at 5:00 or 6:00.

We've had fun getting caught up with and seeing friends, but there's also been much work to do. Besides the usual stuff involved in opening up the house after being gone for six months, we've had the boat to deal with; in my case, mostly unloading it and trying to find storage space for items we've never needed to store before (with no basement). I need to make room in my kitchen for extra food and duplicate containers of everything in the refrigerator. I'm still working on that and expect to make a run to the local food shelf once I get organized. Wayne spent most of yesterday cleaning the outside of the boat—there was already oxidation from the salty air and water—and I'll take care of the inside . . . when I get around to it.

After we finish the boat stuff, it will be time to prepare for Thanksgiving, which we will celebrate November 24th, the Saturday after. Michael and Amy are flying down on Thanksgiving, and our moms, Suzanne, Brian, and Alex will arrive on Friday; they'll be here for five days. Of course, we can hardly wait! It seems much longer than four months since we last saw some of them.

Yesterday we made reservations to fly home to Minnesota on December 5; we'll be there for about a month and will drive back down to Florida in January.

Many thanks to all of you for the "Welcome Home" and "Congratulations" messages.

Friday, November 16, 2007

Spiritual reflections— unplugged and tuned in

The spiritual aspect of this trip was profound. First of all, we felt the power and blessing of your prayers every day, and for that we thank you. As I've mentioned many times, God blessed us with unbelievably superb weather throughout the trip, especially considering it was hurricane season. He kept us safe and healthy (except for two minor visits to the ER) and protected us from countless things that could have gone wrong. I often felt as if he had us wrapped in a protective bubble.

So often in our busy lives it's hard to make room for God. Even if we take time to pray, the communication is mostly one-way because we're immediately on to the next thing and often fail or forget to listen for God's voice. We're busy with work and family obligations, and in our free time we often live in a world of television, radio, iPods, smartphones, computers, and what have you. I think of them as spiritual earplugs—God could be screaming at us and we wouldn't hear him above the noise and distractions. How can we be tuned in to God when we're tuned in to something else? And then we wonder why God doesn't answer our prayers and make his presence known to us.

Except for a very few occasions, Wayne and I went without TV, radio, and newspapers for 3½ months (although this was not by choice). What a blessing that turned out to be! We didn't have a smartphone back then, and because of battery issues, even listening to music was a rare treat. Work was mostly limited to boat stuff, navigation, and trip planning, if you can call that work. Our only family obligation was to keep in touch, which we did by phone, email, and blog. Of course, there's no escaping electronics altogether, even at sea; indeed, the navigation and weather instruments are vital for safety. And of course I did spend quite a bit of time on my computer, blogging and editing photos.

Without all the usual distractions, we learned what it really means to abide in Christ. He was our constant companion and we were always aware of his presence, often spending most of the day just enjoying our Lord's creation and our relationship with him, steeped in his love and peace. We were more "tuned in" to him, which allowed him to guide our travel and protect us to a degree that wouldn't have been possible otherwise. I experienced peace that could only have come from the Holy Spirit in the face of many hair-raising situations, scores of low bridges, and vast expanses of shallow waters. I experienced joy that I didn't even know how to express, which also could only have come from him.

My prayer for everyone reading this is that you too may one day experience the blessing of being "unplugged and tuned in to God." No boat required.

Every day we were blessed and awed by the wonder of God's creation as we experienced it on a deeper level, completely immersed. The variety and beauty of birds, trees, clouds, winds, rocks, terrain, aquatic mammals and fish, sunrises and sunsets, flowers, land creatures, sea shells, water—and of course, homo sapiens—fascinated and delighted us as much on day one and mile one as they did on day 109 and mile 4,630.

God is good . . . all the time.

Stay tuned, there's more to come . . .

Friday, November 16, 2007:

Another world

During the past 109 days, we learned that there's another world out there, fully experienced only from the water, with color, texture, ambience, sensations, and culture so foreign to this Minnesota girl. It is a world of marinas as varied as a Motel 6 is from the Ritz-Carlton, communities on the water where people live, work, play, and socialize, or in our case, simply pass through (they call us "transients").

It is a world whose livelihood is dependent on the sea and where many towns have memorials to honor those lost there. It is a world where fishing boats seem to outnumber cars, and lobster and crab pots seem to outnumber people.

It is a world of peaceful anchorages, wilderness areas, sandy beaches, marshlands, rocky and wooded shores, lighthouses, small fishing villages, beautiful resort towns, large commercial sea ports, all types of housing imaginable, and metropolitan cities—both modern and steeped in history.

It is a world of barges and hardworking tugboats, alert and wary Coast Guard boats, massive freighters and cruise ships, classic and regal-looking tall ships, intimidating war ships, car ferries, tour boats, luxury yachts, lazy trawlers, sleek and high-powered cigarette boats, and recreational sail and power boats of all sizes and descriptions. It is a world of swing bridges, lift bridges, bascule bridges, and of course, 65-foot fixed bridges.

It is a world where the sea is more than just water—it's a living organism with a temperament and personality, a powerful being who can toss us, rage against us, frighten us, delight us, calm us, lull us to sleep, and yes, make us a little queasy. It is a world where whales dominate and inspire awe, seals swim by curiously and inspire humor, dolphins frolic and inspire joy, and manatees bathe lazily and inspire love.

It is a world where people are—well, people—no different from people everywhere, and we smile as we remember them fondly. Each person we met along the way left an imprint on our hearts and made our journey a richer, more textured and colorful experience. There are too many names to mention, but we are grateful to all who contributed to the memories we'll savor of this trip. A special "thank you" goes to those we met en route who joined us on our journey and cheered us on by way of the blog, like Roberta, our good Samaritan in Sault Sainte Marie.

We are so grateful for the privilege of experiencing this other world for the past 3½ months.

Stay tuned, I'm not finished yet . . .

Thursday, November 29, 2007:

I'm still here . . .

I don't know if anyone out there still cares, but I haven't forgotten about doing a final post to the blog. We've been delightfully occupied with company and our Thanksgiving celebration, but everyone's gone now, so I should have time to add to the blog tonight or tomorrow. I hope you all had a blessed Thanksgiving.

Friday, November 30, 2007:

In conclusion . . .

Someone asked me early on what my objectives or goals were for this trip. If you remember what I wrote in the introduction of the book, it shouldn't surprise you to know that I just wanted to make it from beginning to end without abandoning Wayne.

As for the concerns I expressed about the trip at the beginning of this blog:

1) **Fear:** There were only a couple of times when I felt that our safety was in jeopardy; I was more concerned about the boat crashing into a dock or hitting a bridge. Of course, Wayne's sound judgment, caution, and skill at navigation, piloting the boat, and docking cannot be overstated. I was very impressed by that.

2) **Inexperience:** I did very well on the trip and never entertained the thought of flying home (although we'll never know what I would have done on several occasions if a helicopter had shown up and offered me an escape). I became more of an asset to Wayne as time and experience gave me confidence and skill. During dinner one evening, Rachael said something that startled me: "Michele, I know you didn't think of yourself as a sailor when you started this trip, but you sure are a sailor now." Why, yes—I suppose I am!

3) **Lack of interest:** I still don't have a *passion* for sailing and don't enjoy the mechanics of sailing. Having said that, though, I do love to travel on the

boat, visit new places, and spend time outdoors, so I thoroughly enjoyed all the places we visited and sights we saw. And yes, I even enjoyed the sailing . . . tremendously.

4) Homesickness and loneliness: It was a long trip and I wouldn't have wanted it to be any longer. Yes, I missed my land life, but this experience was worth giving it up for 109 days. Although there were some lonely times, we were blessed with visits from family and friends along the way. Traveling with Claus and Rachael came at a time that would have otherwise been the loneliest, as we were in remote areas late in the season and saw few other boats, and the blog and email saved me from being lonely when it was just the two of us.

5) Uncertainties with communication: Communication was seldom an issue. We were pleasantly surprised to have cell phone service probably 90% of the time. We had the satellite phone for backup, but didn't need it much, and we never went more than a few days without internet access.

6) Too much togetherness: Wayne and I did just fine with so much togetherness; we both put maximum effort into making it work and we got along very well. In fact, in response to the many people who asked, it was probably good for our relationship (hmm . . . maybe this retirement thing won't be so bad after all).

The only regret I have is that we left late in the season and had to rush so much. We could have put the trip off until the following spring or done it in segments, but we never considered either option. It would have made for a more leisurely journey, but who knows if it would have been a better journey?

Because I had so many concerns about this trip, the fact that I did it is so much sweeter . . . I guess you could call it a personal victory. The experience reminds me of when I set aside my fear of water to become a certified scuba diver and then went 100 feet deep when I had made up my mind not to go deeper than twenty.

Finally, to those who have faithfully kept up with our blog, or even just checked in periodically, we are humbled and grateful. It means so much to us that you cared enough to take time out of your busy lives to follow our journey and encourage us along the way. I feel a bond with you because it's almost as if you were with us. When people ask, "How was the trip?" I don't know where to start, but I want to say, "Read the blog—it's all there."

We received this email from Mike: "Wayne and Michele, I have to tell you how much I enjoyed reading about your adventures. Checking your blog was quite often the first thing I did when getting to work in the morning. Maybe most of us have had that secret longing for just such an adventure, so for a brief moment each update we could live vicariously through you. Anyway, thank you for sharing your adventures with everyone and God bless both of you. May your seas be calm and bridges be high (at least over 65 feet)."

So there you have it and here I end it. I expected to be seeking out a Twelve Steps group for recovering bloggers, but I'm happy to report that it doesn't look like I'll have a problem. Although there will probably be other blogs for me in the future, it's sad to say good-bye—I miss you already. The *Lena Bea* blog has been, for me, a vital link to all of you, a source of encouragement, an antidote for loneliness, a means of creative expression, and a priceless memoir of our journey, but this chapter is now complete. Thank you for reading.

Life is either a
great adventure
or nothing.

~ Helen Keller

*Man cannot discover
new oceans unless he has
the courage to
lose sight of the shore.*

~ André Gide

Afterword

After things settled down a little we started looking for a dog, and on December 22 Emma (a Havanese puppy) joined  us as a new crew member. Her first trip on *Lena Bea* was in the fall of 2008, when we embarked on a two-week cruise to the Dry Tortugas National Park, about seventy miles west of Key West. That was followed by a two-month trip to the Exuma Cays in the Bahamas for the months of February and March 2009.

In August 2009 we bought a new catamaran, *Chat-Eau*, a Lagoon 380. She wasn't for our personal use, but to put in the charter fleet at Superior Charters in Bayfield, Wisconsin. She was shipped over from France and we, along with Dick Kalow, the owner of Superior Charters, drove out from Minnesota and met her at the dock in Brooklyn, New York. We took her up the Hudson River and the Erie Canal, then stopped in Tonawanda, New York, where Wayne and Dick put up the mast and rigging. Once she was fully commissioned, Dick drove back to Bayfield and John, our friend from Vermilion, Ohio, and a friend of his, another John, joined us in Tonawanda and sailed with us to Vermilion. An old friend, Ray, met us there and completed the trip to Bayfield with us. Of course, we had to stop in Sault Saint Marie for a reunion with Roberta (who worked at Sears and drove Wayne to buy a hose) and her husband, Gary.

We returned to the Exumas for seven weeks in 2011, and went as far south as Duncan Town in the Ragged Islands. We chronicled both Bahamas trips on our blog, *lenabea.blogspot.com*

Tragically, our friend and travel companion, Gary DeSantis, was struck and killed by a car while riding his bicycle on May 19, 2010. My brother Brian succumbed to colon cancer less than two months later on July 9.

After Gary died, Wayne joined forces with Dick and Cindy Kalow at Superior Yachts and took over the Island Packet dealership for the Midwest.

Appendix: About *Lena Bea*

Lena Bea is an Island Packet 445 sailboat. This model has a center cockpit, which makes the cabin spacious with plenty of headroom (6'6" – 6'10"). She is a cutter rig, which means that there is a main sail, a forward sail—called a jib, or genoa—and a sail in between, called a staysail. This combination provides much flexibility in different wind conditions. All sail controls are run to the cockpit for ease of adjustment and safety.

Lena Bea also has an asymmetrical spinnaker, which is a colorful 1400-square-foot sail. This is used in lighter air when going mostly downwind.

In addition to sails, *Lena Bea* is powered by a 75-horsepower Yanmar turbo diesel. She has a Maxiprop feathering propeller that automatically adjusts pitch for optimum thrust in forward or reverse, and keeps the blades straight back when sailing for reduced drag.

Electronics

The heart of the system is two Raymarine E80 displays, one at the helm, and the other at the navigation station. These are eight-inch displays networked together by a Raymarine switch, and are used for a chart plotter (electronic charts and GPS), radar, Sirius weather, and Automatic Identification System (AIS, used for commercial ship identification). The displays are connected to wind, speed, and depth instruments, and provide navigation information and calculations. This equipment is used for route planning, to show current position, and to provide an abundance of information to help with navigation. All of this is integrated with the auto pilot, VHF Radio, a wireless remote, and a Life Tag System.

The auto pilot can steer the boat on a compass heading, by wind angle, or to a waypoint. We use it often to free us up to do other tasks, but one of us is always on watch.

The VHF Radio is our primary means of communication with marinas, other boats, and for local weather information. It has current location information via GPS which can be immediately broadcast in an emergency.

The wireless remote lets us run the auto pilot from anywhere on the boat, and displays other information from the instruments.

The Life Tag System includes wireless devices that we wear. If someone were to fall off while wearing it, an alarm would sound, the position would be captured and displayed, and all navigation automatically changed to the MOB (man overboard) location.

Generator

Lena Bea has an eight-kilowatt Maspower generator powered by a 12.9-horsepower Yanmar diesel. The generator provides electricity that is used for charging batteries, heating water, running electrical outlets, and running the air conditioners/heaters. We have not needed to run it much on this trip.

Inverter

Lena Bea has a Prosine 1800-watt inverter. This provides AC power from the six house batteries. We generally just power the outlets for computers and small appliances.

Batteries and Charging Systems

Almost everything on the boat is powered by 12-volt batteries. There are eight AGM (Absorbed Glass Matt) batteries on *Lena Bea*. These are completely sealed batteries that can function even if inverted, and they can handle a lot of charge/discharge cycles. One battery is dedicated to the engine, one is dedicated to the generator, and six are for the house. They are ninety amp hours each.

Batteries are charged by an electric battery charger, which is powered from shore power or the generator. They are also charged by a high output alternator and regulator when the engine is running. *Lena Bea* has two 130-watt solar panels, which are connected via a Blue Sky controller providing additional battery charging.

Air Conditioning

Lena Bea has two Climma reverse cycle air conditioners. They operate a heat pump, using sea water which is pumped through the systems. A 16,000 BTU system is located in the main salon and also vents to the forward cabin. A 7,000 BTU system is located in the aft cabin (our cabin). They each have a thermostat, and require 120 volts AC, so we need to be on shore power or run the generator to use them.

Water maker

We added a Spectra Ventura 150 water maker in 2009. This allows us to run sea water through a filtering and reverse osmosis process to replenish our water tanks. It can produce about six gallons of water per hour.

Dinghy and Outboard

We have a 10.2-foot Walker Bay Genesis dinghy with a 15-horsepower Honda outboard. We use it to explore and as our taxi for getting us to shore when anchored.

Capacities

Diesel Fuel – 160 gallons

Water – 260 gallons

Hot Water – 10 gallons

Holding Tank – 55 gallons

Links and Resources

Apostle Islands National Lakeshore:
www.nps.gov/apis/index.htm

Bayfield, Wisconsin: bayfield.org

Bay of Fundy: www.bayoffundytourism.com

Cruising Resources: www.waterwayguide.com

Great Lakes: www.great-lakes.net

Intracoastal Waterway: www.atlintracoastal.org and
www.waterwayguide.com

Island Packet Yachts: www.ipy.com

Punta Gorda boating: www.boat2puntagorda.com

Punta Gorda tourism:
www.visitflorida.com/Punta_Gorda

Quebec: www.bonjourquebec.com

Sailing glossary: www.sailinglinks.com/glossary.htm

Saint Lawrence Seaway: www.seaway.dot.gov
www.great-lakes.net/lakes/stlaw.html

Sirius Marine Weather:
www.siriusxm.com/marineweather

Superior Charters: superiorcharters.com

Superior Yachts: superioryachts.com

Thousand Islands: www.visit1000islands.com/visitorinfo

Tidal Bore: bayoffundy.com/about/tidal-bore
www.tidalbore.info

Welland Canal: www.wellandcanal.com

Whales: animals.nationalgeographic.com/animals/mammals/blue-whale

Whales in St. Lawrence Seaway:
www.bonjourquebec.com/qc-en/baleines0.html

Books and Cruising Guides

Chapman Piloting & Seamanship 65th Edition, Elbert S. Maloney; Hearst, September 28, 2006

Superior Way: The Cruising Guide to Lake Superior, by Bonnie Dahl; Lake Superior Port Cities, 3rd edition (June 1, 2001)

Dozier's Waterway Guide Great Lakes 2006, Ryan Stallings (editor), published by Jack Dozier (February 15, 2006)

Lake Superior Chartbook + Cruising Guide, Richardson's Marine Publishing

Lake Huron Chartbook + Cruising Guide, Richardson's Marine Publishing

Lake Erie Chartbook + Cruising Guide, Richardson's Marine Publishing

Lake Ontario Chartbook + Cruising Guide, Richardson's Marine Publishing

Cruising Guide St. Lawrence River and Quebec Waterways, published by L'Escale Nautique

Maptech Embassy Cruising Guide: New England Coast, Richardson's Marine Publishing

Dozier's Waterway Guide Mid-Atlantic 2007: Chesapeake Bay and the ICW to Georgia, Ryan Stallings (editor), published by Dozier Media Group

Maptech Embassy Cruising Guide: Chesapeake Bay to Florida, Richardson's Marine Publishing

Dozier's Waterway Guide Southern 2007: Florida, the Gulf of Mexico and the Bahamas, Gary Reich (editor), published by Dozier Media Group

Maptech Embassy Cruising Guide: Florida, Richardson's Marine Publishing

Cruising Guide to Eastern Florida, Claiborne Young, Pelican Publishing Company

Cruising Guide to Western Florida, Claiborne Young, Pelican Publishing Company

*My prayer for everyone
reading this is that you too
may one day experience
the blessing of being
"unplugged and tuned in to God."
No boat required.*

~ Michele McClintock Sharp

About the Authors

Michele calls herself a retired stay-at-home mom. She worked for a photography studio in downtown Minneapolis for a few years, mostly as a wedding photographer, and later did some freelance portrait work. She gave up professional photography when she realized she was losing the joy of taking pictures; Michele wanted to be able to photograph their children without it feeling like a "job." She finds the most joy while photographing nature.

Wayne is a partly-retired businessman who began his career with IBM. He bought his own computer-related business in 1983 and sold it in 2006, when the perfect exit opportunity came along. He continues to dabble in a few business ventures and occasionally serves as a charter captain for Superior Charters. He, along with Dick and Cindy Kalow of Superior Yachts, own the Island Packet dealership for the Midwest.

You can read about their sailing experience on page 118.

Wayne and Michele live in Punta Gorda, Florida, for most of the year, and spend their summers close to family in Plymouth, Minnesota.

Email:
reluctantsailor@me.com

Website:
reluctantsailor.net

Facebook:
facebook.com/ReluctantSailor

Twitter:
@SailorReluctant

Blog:
lenabea.blogspot.com